Everything I Needed to Know
I Learned AFTER Law School

Second Edition

Everything I Needed to Know I Learned AFTER Law School

Memos to a Young Family Lawyer

M. Sue Talia

Second Edition

EVERYTHING I NEEDED TO KNOW I LEARNED AFTER LAW SCHOOL: MEMOS TO A YOUNG FAMILY LAWYER

SECOND EDITION

Copyright 2016 by M. Sue Talia and Nexus Publishing Company
All rights reserved.

Nexus Publishing Company
P.O. Box 2335
Danville, CA 94526-7335

ISBN 10: 0965107582
ISBN 13: 9780965107587
Library of Congress Control Number: 2016909272
Nexus Publishing Company, Danville, CA

For more information, contact Nexus Publishing Company, nexusbooks.com

Although the author and publisher have made every effort to ensure the accuracy and completeness of the information contained in this book, we assume no responsibility for errors, inaccuracies, omissions, or any inconsistency herein. Any slights of people, places or organizations are unintentional.

Printed in the United States of America

Other Books by the Author

How to Avoid the Divorce From Hell
(and dance together at your daughter's wedding)

Unbundling Your Divorce:
How to Find a Lawyer to Help You Help Yourself

Uncoupling in Three-Quarter Time:
Life-Affirming Divorce Poetry

Dedication

To Marty and Gus, who had no personal or professional investment in me. Nevertheless, each recognized a promising young lawyer lacking proper guidance and took it upon himself to volunteer his wisdom and experience at a key point in my early career. They pointed me in the right direction, saved me much trial and error, and encouraged me to take the high road. I bless the memory of both of them, and hope that by this handbook I am passing on in some small measure the profound gift they gave to me.

Table of Contents

Preface · xv

One   What Kind of Lawyer Do You Want to Be? · · · · · · · · · · · · · · · 1
      Why be a family lawyer at all? · 1
      What kind of clients do you want? · 3
      What do you want the colleagues you
      respect to say about you? · 4
      It's always showtime · 5
      What do you want the judges you respect
      to say about you? · 6
      How to find a mentor · 7
      What if *your* boss is that idiot, who happens
      to sign the paychecks? · 9
      When to do it your own way · 10
      Do I have to work 60 hour weeks? · 10
      You are always judged by the company you keep · · · · · · · · · · 11
      You don't get a second chance to build a
      professional reputation · 12
Two   Office Mechanics and Work Habits · 13
      Setting up your physical office · 13
      Technology is your friend · 15
      Forms and templates or, reinventing the wheel · · · · · · · · · · · 17
      Checklists, outlines and other time saving tools · · · · · · · · · · 18
      Fee agreements · 19
      Confidentiality · 19

	Sharing office space ·	·21
	Know your limitations ·	22
	Phone Calls and Emails ·	22
	How to paper your file ·	·23
	The ugly green monster on the corner of your desk · · · · · · ·	·25
Three	Learning Your Craft ·	·27
	What is an advocate, anyway? ·	·27
	Why it is important to develop a case plan and how to do it ·	28
	Personal research files ·	30
	Weaknesses??? WHAT weaknesses? · · · · · · · · · · · · · · · · ·	30
	The importance of being consistently professional · · · · · · · ·	·31
	Distinguishing a gripe from a legal issue · · · · · · · · · · · · · ·	·32
	How many cases at a time is enough? · · · · · · · · · · · · · · · · ·	·33
	Expert witnesses ·	34
	Learn almost as much as your expert knows · · · · · · · · · · ·	34
	The Expert "Lawyer Wannabe" ·	34
	Protecting your experts ·	·35
	Taking depositions ·	·35
	Preparing your client for his deposition and testimony · · · · ·	·37
	When to line up your witnesses ·	·38
	Oops! Tomorrow's the settlement conference · · · · · · · · · · · ·	·39
	Never underestimate your opponent · · · · · · · · · · · · · · · · · ·	·39
	The difference between "real" time and "lawyer" time · · · · ·	40
	Cross examination isn't a refresher course · · · · · · · · · · · · ·	40
	How to ask a question and other no-brainers they don't teach you in law school · · · · · · · · · · · · · · · · ·	·41
	I just got out of law school. Why do I have to do CLE? · · · ·	42
	How to know when you're out of your depth and what to do about it ·	43
Four	Finding and Screening Clients ·	44
	What kind of clients do you want, anyway? · · · · · · · · · · · ·	44
	Building referral sources ·	46

Other lawyers · 46

Other marketing tools ·47

The blind date: client screening and
the initial interview ·49

Why it's sometimes a good thing to tell a client
your strengths and weaknesses (after you've
figured out what they are) ·51

Concluding the Interview ·53

When (and how) to turn a client away · · · · · · · · · · · · · · 54

Why refusing to accept a client who wanted to write
me a big check that day was one of the smartest
client development moves I ever made · · · · · · · · · · · · · · ·57

How not to reject a client· ·58

Five   Keeping Clients · 60

Setting Boundaries· ·61

Accessibility issues ·62

Hand holding ·63

How to keep communication flowing · · · · · · · · · · · · · · · 64

Tools for success with the disorganized client· · · · · · · · · · · ·65

What do you mean there are weaknesses in my case? · · · · · · · 66

Nine things NEVER to say to a client · · · · · · · · · · · · · · ·67

Things never to say about a client to someone else
(especially the judge) ·69

How to refuse to do something a client wants you to do · · · ·71

What if you're getting sucked into the client's
agenda and losing your objectivity? · · · · · · · · · · · · · · · · ·72

How much of my strategy should I share with my client?· · · ·73

It seems obvious, but never lie · · · · · · · · · · · · · · · · · · ·74

Discussing other cases with your client · · · · · · · · · · · · · ·74

Give clients bad news verbally and personally · · · · · · · · · · ·74

"Strong letter to follow"· ·75

Swapping jokes in chambers· ·75

What to do when you see clients in public · · · · · · · · · · · · ·76

Prepare anything which requires the client's
signature well in advance ·76
What to do with the client who tries to bully you · · · · · · · · 77

Six   Firing Clients ·79
How to recognize the problem client and
what to do about it ·79
When and how to fire a client ·82
What if you really detest your client? · · · · · · · · · · · · · · · · ·83
The most dangerous client there is · · · · · · · · · · · · · · · · · · ·85
How to spot the Client from Hell · · · · · · · · · · · · · · · · · ·85

Seven You and Your Staff · 90
How much staff do I really need? · · · · · · · · · · · · · · · · · · · 90
How much do I pay them? · 90
The Gospel According to Aretha ·91
Training isn't optional ·92
NEVER blame your staff for your own screw up · · · · · · · · ·92
Share the windfall ·93
Do your own work in a timely manner · · · · · · · · · · · · · · · ·93
Remember that you can learn from your staff · · · · · · · · · · 94
They have a life, too ·95
What if you have no control over staff? · · · · · · · · · · · · · · · 96
What if the staff treats you like the new kid
on the block? · 96
The Office Manager from Hell · 97

Eight Opposing Counsel ·98
What about opposing counsel? ·98
Opposing counsel is the enemy, right? · · · · · · · · · · · · · · · ·98
Demonizing the other side · 99
What goes around comes around · 99
Never complain about your own client to
opposing counsel ·100
The wages of "war stories" ·100
What to do about "he said/she said" letters · · · · · · · · · · · ·100
The importance of professional courtesies · · · · · · · · · · · · ·101

What to do with opposing counsel who tries
to bully or intimidate you ·102
How to know when life is just too short to
deal with a particular opponent ·102

Nine   You, The Judges and Court Staff ·104
Always be courteous and professional · · · · · · · · · · · · · · · · ·104
Why it is important to thank the judge who
just handed you a part of your anatomy· · · · · · · · · · · · · · · · ·104
Promises, Promises· ·105
Who is making the decision, anyway? · · · · · · · · · · · · · · · · ·105
How to read the judge and what to do when
you're losing him ·106
How to get on the judge's blacklist· · · · · · · · · · · · · · · · · · · ·107
When it's ok to ask to talk with the judge at
the conclusion of a case and how to do it · · · · · · · · · · · · · ·108
How to handle the judge who tries to bully you
into sacrificing your client ·109
What about the judge's staff?· ·110

Ten   Killing Trees: How to do Good Paperwork · · · · · · · · · · · · · ·111
We aren't paid by the word any more· · · · · · · · · · · · · · · · · ·111
A leads to B leads to C leads to success · · · · · · · · · · · · · · · ·111
All arguments aren't created equal ·112
Eliminate extraneous facts· ·112
Always check your authorities ·113
How to prepare exhibits the judge will love · · · · · · · · · · · ·113
Never put dangerous or confidential facts
in a public record· ·114
Review spells success ·115

Eleven   Billing and Collecting Fees ·116
Rule #1: It doesn't matter how many hours you bill · · · · · · ·116
What if you work for a firm which sets a
quota for billable hours?· ·116
How to bill ·117
When not to bill ·120

When to reduce a bill ·120
How to talk to a client about money · · · · · · · · · · · · ·121
How not to do it ·123
"It's not the money; it's the principle" · · · · · · · · · · · ·124
How to be sure you get paid · · · · · · · · · · · · · · · · · ·125
When to take it on faith ·126
How to deal with the case that turns sour · · · · · · · · · ·128
The clash between crusades and business · · · · · · · · · · ·129
What happens when you get burned on fees?
(and you will) ·129
How to stay out of fee arbitration · · · · · · · · · · · · · · ·130
The deadbeat client ·132
How to win at fee arbitration · · · · · · · · · · · · · · · · · ·133
What if the person you work for only gives
you lousy cases to work on? · · · · · · · · · · · · · · · · · · ·134

Twelve   The Hard Stuff ·135
What to do when you think you've screwed up · · · · · · ·135
You haven't a clue how to do something
you need to do ·136
What if you are really stuck and don't have
an in-house mentor? ·136
What if the person who is paying your
bill isn't the client? ·137
What if your client wants you do to
something you feel is inappropriate? · · · · · · · · · · · · · ·138
What if your boss instructs you to do something
you don't think is ethical? ·138
What if you're well into the case and realize
that your client really is "the bad guy"? · · · · · · · · · · · ·138
The family you can't fix ·139
Protecting yourself ·140

Thirteen   Your Legacy ·143

About the Author ·147

Preface

So you've passed the Bar. You've gotten your ticket punched. Now what? You know lots of law, most of it irrelevant to the specific field you intend to enter. And you probably haven't a clue how to go about *practicing* law. All that stuff they taught you in law school doesn't seem very useful when you have to GPS directions to the courthouse and can't get the clerk to accept your paperwork for filing when you get there.

Where do you start, and how do you learn your craft? There are lots of mediocre lawyers out there, and you don't want to be one of them. The comments which follow are directed at family lawyers, but also apply to any form of law in which you regularly interact with the public consumer of legal services.

How do you learn to do it right from the beginning, *before* you've developed bad habits and are too busy to unlearn them? Here's how. Let's get started.

One

What Kind of Lawyer Do You Want to Be?

Why be a family lawyer at all?

What is it that draws you to family law? Presumably you enjoy dealing with people. If not, you may want to rethink your career choice and direct your attention to areas of the law which focus more on documents and abstract concepts. There's plenty of both in family law, but that's not where you'll spend most of your time. You will be on the front lines, dealing with families in crisis. In the trenches, as it were. Only criminal lawyers spend more time in court. Even those who call themselves "civil litigators" probably spend less time in court than you will. So, what does it take to become a successful family law advocate?

Take some time to think about how you define your role as an advocate. Do you see yourself as a problem solver? A negotiator? A gladiator? A crusader? You will attract very different clients, depending on how you answer this question.

There are certain constants in family law that you will need to be aware of. First, you must like people. You'll be seeing them at their very worst, in emotional crisis. This can be both wearing and immensely satisfying, especially when you know that you played a positive role in helping them through it.

1

You also have to be able to handle conflict. It sounds weird for a lawyer to be uncomfortable with conflict, but many fields of practice have remarkably little of it. You'll have lots. It's surprising how many lawyers aren't good at it, and substitute rudeness for professionalism and stridency for advocacy, or who show tummy at the first sign of stiff opposition.

You need to think quickly and be good in court. Not all lawyers do, but you will. This specialty is not for the shy and retiring who don't like public speaking and can't think on their feet.

You need to be analytical and objective. Your clients generally can't analyze their own situations. They are too close to their problems to do so effectively, so you'll have to do it for them, and their legal problems can be amazingly complex.

You must be well organized and able to separate relevant information from the irrelevant (most of which your client will think is *critically* important). You'll be presented with stacks of raw data and must be able to organize, analyze and present it in an intelligible fashion.

In addition to all of this, you need to know a lot about many other areas of the law as well. You must know about real estate, because you'll be dividing property and negotiating property sales. You have to know finance, because you'll be tracing property transactions, income and expenses. You'll have to know how to read and interpret a tax return and how to spot red flags, because sometimes you'll be presented with bogus tax returns. You need to know about stock options and deferred compensation, including both the state and federal rules which govern them, because you'll be faced with these issues in case after case. You have to learn about business valuation, because you'll do a lot of it. And you'll need to know practical psychology. Even if you don't intend to do custody work, you'll be practicing some psychology every time you interact with your client, the other attorney, the opposing party, or the judge.

And finally, you'll have to develop all the *other* skills of effective trial lawyers: the ability to take a good deposition, mastery of the rules of evidence, direct and cross examination, negotiation, document preparation and analysis.

And you'll do all of this with people who are in the middle of one of the most emotionally distressing events the legal system is ever called upon to address. You'll be doing it with too little access to courts, frequently inadequate litigation budgets, and tremendous time and financial pressures.

At the same time you are learning your craft, you also need to learn how to leave it at the office, to protect your personal time and space. Otherwise, it will eat you alive.

You have to like this process, with all its inadequacies, or you won't last long. The good news is that it is possible to develop the necessary skills in a reasonable time, and this field of law can be one of the most satisfying (if sometimes frustrating) of specialties. To succeed, take some time to think about why you are drawn to it in the first place, and what kind of practice you want to have ten years from now.

What kind of clients do you want?

Clients come in all shapes and sizes. As you experience different sorts, you'll learn to spot those with whom you communicate best as well as the ones who drive you nuts. It is important to start making these distinctions as soon as you begin collecting the data on which to make them, i.e., as soon as you start representing real people in real family law matters. Remember, happy clients send you their friends. If you do it well, you are likely to get more of the same. You'll learn that certain careers attract similar personality types. And, of course, everyone talks about his or her divorce constantly at work and with their friends. That means that if a client likes you, you are likely to get referrals of similar cases. If you relate well to peace officers or firefighters, you may build a whole practice around representing them. Or engineers. Or airline pilots. Or teachers.

If you want to represent "high end" types (those with lots of money and complex estates and legal issues), you'd better learn a lot about finance, business and tax. Business people want lawyers who speak their language, even when the legal problem is personal (or maybe most especially then.)

As you look around the courthouse at other lawyers, make a note of the lawyers you would like to emulate and the kinds of cases you'd like to ultimately have, and ask yourself what specific skills or talents will make you more attractive to that kind of client. Then, go out and develop the skills.

What do you want the colleagues you respect to say about you?

This is where you start thinking about your professional reputation and how you start building your practice.

Suppose you want to be one of the heavy hitters, but you're just out of law school, you've hung out your own shingle, and have no ability yet to move in those circles. You can still introduce yourself to the big shots at family law functions, and most of them will be kind and courteous, at least for a few minutes. Don't monopolize them, but let them know you're out there.

Be aware of who is sitting in the back of the courtroom as you are putting on your case. We all watch each other, whether consciously or not and, without missing a beat in running through our own upcoming presentation, we judge who is doing a good job, who shows promise, and who can't cross-examine her way out of a paper bag. Pay attention to what lawyers say about each other. That's the first clue to deciding what reputation you want to build. It doesn't happen in a vacuum, and if you have a clear picture of how you want to be regarded professionally, you're more likely to create the reputation you want.

If you get a chance to go up against an "A" list attorney early in your legal career, don't panic. It's a blessing. Do the best damn job you can in the most professional way. It could be the best referral source you ever have. Most of the top family lawyers take only a fraction of the cases referred to them, because they have earned the right to be selective. If they think you are a promising up-and-comer, they may refer one of their rejects to you, and their handoffs can be very nice, indeed, thank you. And if they send you a difficult case or difficult client, assume you are being tested and it is an audition. If you do a lousy job, the source of that referral is likely to call Ms. Big Shot and report. The reverse is also true, and word will soon get back to her that it is safe to refer to you and you'll handle the matter competently.

It's always showtime

Lawyers are always judging each other. Unlike many other professionals, much of what we do is in public, in front of a critical, often egocentric, and sometimes hostile group of our peers. A therapist once confided in me that she thought I was lucky to have that peer observation as part of my profession; she felt she always worked in private in a vacuum, and would have loved the opportunity to watch and be critiqued by others in her field. Well, that is an advantage of our profession. It is also a reason to never turn in a sloppy hearing. You never know who is watching. This doesn't just apply to newbies. I remember sitting in the back of the court room watching a couple of old timers who had been doing this work so long, they could do it in their sleep – and it showed. It was clear that they were just mailing it in, rather than really doing the good job for their clients that I knew they both were capable of. I swore on the spot that I'd never be one of them.

And speaking of never knowing who is watching, that includes the attorney sitting on the next bench at the courthouse, apparently reading a file while you explain the settlement offer and your recommendations to your client. I've revised my opinion of a number of attorneys (both up and down) based on my observations of how they handled their clients or opposing counsel in the hallway at the courthouse when they thought no one was listening.

Ask yourself who in your legal community is doing it the way you want to. When I was a young lawyer, I identified a couple of local attorneys who had the kind of practice I wanted to have some day. I loved it when one of them was on calendar the same day I had a hearing and I could watch how they did it. Never consider it a waste of time to sit in the back of the courtroom watching other attorneys putting on their cases as you wait for yours to be called. It's a wonderful learning opportunity, and your client is paying you to do it. Study those lawyers every chance you get. Notice who is smoothly getting evidence admitted and who is struggling to frame a question. Notice who has a calm, professional demeanor and who has watched too many courtroom shows on TV. Make a mental note of everything you think was effective and everything that wasn't. And of course, watch the judge to see what tactics seem to be working.

And as you're doing this, remember that the point of good lawyering is to get the best possible result for your client, which frequently requires no more than making good use of the limited trial time you have. There are no brownie points for reducing the opposing client to tears just to show that you can, or for gratuitous grandstanding, which just irritates the judge and wastes precious time. When you see someone you think did an effective job, ask yourself what made it effective, and how you might incorporate that technique at your next opportunity.

Note the attorneys who joke with opposing counsel at the expense of their own clients. It may be tempting as a new attorney to do the same. After all, they are your colleagues and you want them to like you. *Don't do it.* Listen to what attorneys you respect say about their clients, their opponents and the judges. Whom do *they* respect? Why?

Be glad that other, more experienced lawyers are sitting in the back of the courtroom watching you put on your hearing. And if you're really, really lucky, someday a kindly older "A List" lawyer will follow you out of the courtroom, buy you a cup of coffee, and gently tell you how you could do it better next time. Someone did that for me once, and this book is dedicated to him.

What do you want the judges you respect to say about you?

This is a corollary to the last section. It goes without saying that you want judges to respect you as a professional. All too many lawyers translate this into "schmoozing" with the judge. It isn't about who can tell the best joke to get the judge laughing…don't take that road! If you really want the judge's good opinion, you have to earn it with solid, professional performance. *Then* you can tell a joke or two, if appropriate.

Here's an instructive story. I was once on a commission charged with vetting applicants for judicial appointments. Also on the commission was a fine trial judge from my county. The name of one of my colleagues came up as a possible appointee, and the judge immediately volunteered that this attorney had tried a single civil case before him eight or nine years before. He clearly remembered the concise, professional way the attorney handled the case and the fact that before trial started, the judge thought he didn't have a much of a case. By the end of the trial, the attorney in question had completely changed the judge's opinion and prevailed on all points.

At an appropriate time, I took the opportunity to pass this compliment on to my colleague, who was stunned that this fine judge had such a clear memory of a single trial so many years before, and had retained the positive impression for so long.

I always wanted to be the attorney the judge called when his own son or daughter or a personal friend had a family law problem. I can't think of a better compliment. And I didn't get those referrals because I told jokes in chambers. I got them because he liked the way I handled my cases when I appeared before him. Some of my best cases came to me because a judge thought highly of my work.

How to find a mentor

Of course, you want to learn at the knee of a master, someone who has exactly the kind of practice you want and who can teach you how to build your own. Most of us aren't so lucky. As you start to interact with other, more experienced attorneys, ask them how they got started, what they did that really helped them, what they wish they had done differently. Don't do this on your client's time, of course. Most good attorneys are grateful for the help they received on the way up and are willing to pass some of it along to a bright young lawyer who is eager to learn. Take advantage of that. And don't forget to ask the most important question of all: "What are the mistakes that new lawyers make most frequently and how can I avoid them?"

Attend the meetings of your bar association's family law groups and meet as many of the more experienced lawyers as possible. Ask them the same questions and make mental note of their answers. Learn to distinguish the egocentric blowhard who takes this as an opportunity to bore you to death with inflated tales of his exploits "in the old days" from the person who is willing to share experiences and lessons in a way that is constructive and helpful to you.

When you attend your local bar association and practice section meetings, sit at a different table each time. Let the more experienced attorneys know you are out there. Get involved in committee work in your local bar. That is a great way to get known. Of course, it goes without saying that you should do excellent committee work. Be sure you always follow through on what you promise to do. That will show the other members that you can be counted on to do the same for the clients they might refer to you in the future.

Find one or two experienced attorneys with whom you connect and ask them if you can occasionally call them, meet them for lunch or buy some of their time to pick their brains. This book came out of one of those arrangements. I met a young woman at a social event and realized she was a bright up-and-comer who was unfortunately working for an idiot. We connected immediately. Sometime later, she called and asked me if she could occasionally run issues by me if she didn't make a pest of herself. For the next year or so, she would occasionally call to set up a time to talk. I was happy to oblige, and ultimately she had enough confidence to leave the idiot and go out on her own. When I decided to write a book about mentoring, I sent the first draft of the manuscript to her and asked her to look at it from the perspective of a new lawyer and tell me what additional issues I should cover.

If you find someone willing to be a resource, use their time wisely. Decide in advance what questions you want to ask and what information you need. If you meet them for lunch, pick up the check. Sometimes the offer will be declined because they remember how tight the budget was at the beginning, and if so, accept graciously and insist on picking it up yourself the next time.

What if *your* boss is that idiot, who happens to sign the paychecks?

This happens to many new lawyers. You are thrilled to be hired by an experienced family lawyer, so you won't have to learn your craft on the fly. She looks and sounds good. She has lots of clients, so she must be good, right? After all, how are you supposed to know who is good and who is not, especially if the person who hired you *seems* to know their stuff (and they *all* seem to when you don't know anything yourself). Then you find out that the person who is training you barely made the "C" list, when you are aiming for the "A" list and a Martindale-Hubbell av Preeminent rating.

Brainless twits are out there, a testament to the fact that sometimes family law litigants don't know they've been badly represented, because they don't know how much better they would have done with a really good lawyer. So they keep sending their friends to their lawyer, and pretty soon someone who talks the talk but practices at a mediocre level has developed a relatively successful practice. That's not who you want to be. You want to be recognized as someone who knows what he's doing and is at the top of his game. And fresh out of law school, *everyone* knows more than you do. It is easy to make a mistake and think you're starting out in a good office, only to find that your boss is the laughing stock of his colleagues. Follow the suggestions for finding a mentor and find some experienced and respected attorneys to whom you can turn in a pinch for guidance.

Sometimes it is instructive to see how it *shouldn't* be done, assuming you know the difference. Of course, even a jerk knows how to do *some* things right, so don't just assume that doing the opposite is better. Continue to watch the good lawyers and emulate their approach when appropriate. Ask yourself who is respected by the bar? Who is liked, but not necessarily respected? Which do you want to be? It's harder, but you can still learn now to practice competently, even if you don't have a good role model in the office.

When to do it your own way

Suppose you are working as an associate for a more experienced lawyer. Of course, you want to learn as much as possible. But what if the way your boss is telling you to do something doesn't seem right? Well, that's a tough one. Of course, he is your boss, and you're being paid to follow instructions. And, of course, you don't have anything to measure it against; this is the first legal job you've had.

If your boss's viewpoint still doesn't feel right, ask yourself if it is a question of ethics, style, or work habits. You'll need to use a different analysis for each. If its ethics, it's a no-brainer. Read the Rules of Professional Conduct, and adhere to them to the letter.

If it's style or work habits, try your boss's methods for a while. If they increase your efficiency, make things run more smoothly and promote good client or office relations, they're keepers. If not, start experimenting with other methods which work better.

Do I have to work 60 hour weeks?

Here's some good news. No, you don't. It's ok to want a life *and* a practice. The legal culture is changing because more professionals are insisting on simultaneously having a family, hobbies and a legal career and giving neither of them short shrift. The big firms will probably continue to follow the old rules, but even some of them are finding that it is no longer their grandfather's practice of law. Also, with the increasing specialization of family law, it is far more likely you will find even the very top family lawyers in small firms or sole practice. Family law lends itself to such a structure, and doesn't fit particularly well with the mega firm mentality.

You'll be working longer hours at the beginning, of course, because you're just learning your profession, and you need to be willing to invest the time to learn it well. Lots of what you do at the beginning will be on your own time and not the client's.

I was never a fan of working nights and weekends, even in the "old days" when that was the norm in the firm where I worked[1]. For one thing, our work is simply too stressful to not give ourselves a breather. We can't continue to bring the same quality to our work if we don't. What is important is to do good work, and always be sure you give your clients (and your boss, if you have one) value received.

You are always judged by the company you keep

Lawyers are notorious gossips and love telling war stories. They always discuss opponents with each other, usually in a way that makes them look better than the opposition. Don't give them a story to tell.

This comes up all the time. Whenever an attorney starts a case against an unknown opponent, she calls a colleague to ask if they have heard of the new kid on the block, or had any dealings with them. They'll want to know what kind of experience it was. They will want to know who you trained with, how professional you were, and anything else that will give them a clue what to expect in their interaction with you. From your very first interaction with opposing attorneys, you want the impression you left with them to be professional. And suppose you started out with a bad first choice of mentor? If they hear "She started out working for Curtis Slimeball," that can be a killer unless it is followed up with "but she got out of there pretty quickly, and she's always been straight with me." By the same token, if they think you tried to pull a fast

---

1　And don't kid yourself about what goes on in many of these offices on Saturday. Of course, *some* work got done. In my firm, they counted the cars in the parking lot on Saturday morning as a test of which associates were more dedicated to advancement. Mine was rarely there. However, it was there often enough for me to know that the people who bragged about working every weekend spent a lot of time on Saturday mornings discussing the upcoming Super Bowl, or telling war stories, rather than on real work.

one or acted unprofessionally, that will come out as well. If the advice they get when they inquire about you is "watch your back," you're toast.

You don't get a second chance to build a professional reputation

You start developing your professional reputation with your first client, your first case, your first contact with opposing counsel, your first appearance before a judge. It's easier to start out right than it is to undo a bad start or try a do over. Make sure that the people with whom you interact professionally start to recognize you as someone who projects the qualities for which you want to be known in the future.

In practice, there's *nothing* that is ultimately more important than your professional reputation. Never compromise it, risk it for a client, or for *any* other reason.

Two

Setting up your physical office

E ven if your office is a cubbyhole off the library, it should be neat and professional.

Put a clock where you can see it as you are talking to your client. That way, you learn to keep accurate time and billing records while maintaining eye contact.

If you don't have a window with a nice view, put a picture of something you like where you can look at it. You'll be spending a lot of time in your office, and it should be a pleasant place for you. Don't put your diplomas on the wall opposite your desk. *You* know where you went to law school. It's the client who needs to see them, so put them on the wall behind you, and put a picture you like opposite your desk and behind your client chairs where you can see it. And as soon as you've developed enough professionally not to need diplomas for credibility, put them in the hall, in the waiting room or somewhere else. Before I took my own diplomas down entirely, I put them behind the door, so they were visible when the door was closed and I was with a client, and I didn't have to look at them the rest of the time. And do have them professionally framed. The schlock frame from the dime store creates the impression of dime store service. That's not the image you want to project.

Put a picture with special meaning next to your computer monitor. It's best if it reminds you why you are doing this work:

- Your family
- The vacation you'd love to have
- The secluded beach where you'd like to have a beach house some day
- Whatever else motivates you

Don't leave stacks of files around your office. You may mean to convey the impression that you're so good that you're very, very busy. That's not the message it sends. Instead, it creates the impression that you are disorganized and there's lots of stuff you're not doing. Clients with any sense probably will wonder how long *their* file will sit on the floor before you get around to it. It's simply unprofessional. It may even be a breach of confidentiality if your other clients' names are visible to the casual observer.

Never leave one client's file, phone messages, correspondence, or other documents where another client or opposing counsel can see them. You'll learn how to read upside down soon enough. Never forget that you aren't the only one who can do it.

Boxes of client files in the conference room are a breach of client confidentiality. Lots of people have potential access. The client's name may be written on the box. I remember one attorney's conference room where there were several boxes stacked in the corner labeled "Jones Crap" except the name wasn't Jones but an unusual and locally well known surname. Everyone who saw those boxes (including the client himself, if he attended a meeting in that room) had a good idea how that lawyer felt about his case. I saw those boxes in the same place for well over a year as I had a series of depositions and meetings in that room, and I'll bet every one of that lawyer's clients who saw them wondered if the attorney considered his case "crap" also. Don't do it, even if file storage space is scarce. Find another place and never use a pejorative term in the file label. In fact, never leave one client's name on a box or file that is visible by any other client or opposing counsel.

Technology is your friend

Your computer is your most important piece of equipment. You'll use it for everything from running support guidelines and filling out court forms to doing legal research and e-mailing clients. Buy the best one you can afford with the fastest chip and biggest, baddest hard drive available. You'll fill it up fast enough. Make sure it has a top of the line sound card so you can use speech recognition software. Accuracy has improved dramatically, and it's a lot cheaper than paying staff to transcribe dictation. It will make your work much more efficient. Similarly, if you are using speech recognition, you will need a microphone designed specifically for that purpose. Buy the best one you can find (usually *not* the one that came with the software). With more work being done by email, both with clients and opposing counsel, it is an incredible timesaver to be able to simply dictate your email right into the computer.

Computerize your client conflicts lists and keep the database current. Right now, you don't have many cases and remember everyone who has consulted with you. You won't in the future. And it's particularly a problem in family law where people frequently use different names or go through a series of marriages and divorces. There's no excuse not to have conflicts and other databases up to date and at your fingertips.

Use good timekeeping software. There are demo disks you can download for free. Try them out and find which works best for you. It's a good idea to input your time directly into a computer rather than rely on paper timesheets which you must pay someone else to input later. Train yourself to input your time immediately and use the timer built into your software.

Do your billing in house. Do not use a billing service which only allows you to send bills at certain times of the month. It is cheap and easy to do your billing on your own computer, and being able to print up to the minute bills will make for more effective fee requests and increase the likelihood that your bill is paid in full on presentation.

There are lots of law specific programs which allow you to enter client information once and then insert it into a legal document with the click of a mouse. Find one and learn to use it. It will save you untold time and after all, to an attorney, time *is* money.

Get a cordless hands free telephone headset. I couldn't function without mine. They are a godsend when you have a long case management conference call with the court, or telephone call with your client. It leaves your hands free to take notes. And if it is cordless, you can wander into the file room to find the piece of paper you need to answer the question. Also, if your headset is properly configured, you can switch back and forth between the telephone and your speech recognition software without taking the headset off.

Learn how to do your own word processing, how to prepare a good spreadsheet, and set up and use a database. Doing some of (or even the majority of) your own computer work is neither unprofessional nor demeaning. You'll do much better work if you understand the ins and outs of what you are doing, and the only way to do that is hands on. Even if you have ample staff *you* need to know how to do everything that *they* do. More about that later. And while we're talking about technology, see that your staff has cordless headsets as well. It will vastly increase their efficiency.

Develop a consistent and logical protocol for naming and organizing files and subfiles, both of the paper variety and on your hard drive. Write down your file naming protocol so your staff knows to follow it consistently. This will save much time in tracking down the errant pleading or discovery request.

And, of course, back up your data, back up your data, back up your data, and store the most recent copy offsite.

Forms and templates or, reinventing the wheel

These are your stock in trade. Don't start from scratch each time you draft something. Instead, develop a database of forms and templates which can be tailored on a case by case basis. Then keep them current as the laws change.

Borrow from well drafted documents that come across your desk. If you're going to use a whole document, do give the drafter a courtesy call and ask if he minds. He usually won't object, but it's the right thing to do. After all, he probably spent a lot of time developing that prenuptial agreement form.

As you tailor your forms for a specific client, add a little to your actual drafting time for billing purposes. That's how you recoup the time you spend drafting and updating forms. It's a legitimate charge because this client is getting the benefit of work you did developing and modifying the form. That's part of the service you are providing and for which you should be paid.[2]

Keep the forms in a separate directory on your computer for easy access. It's a pain in the rear to try to remember the name of the last case on which you prepared a particular document so you can revise it for your current client. It wastes your and your staff's time to track them down. Besides, the other case file may be closed and in storage, and how is that going to help you get your pleading on file tomorrow? Train yourself to always work from a clean form rather than tailoring one client's document for another. Doing this just increases the risk that you will fail to edit out some client-specific data. Not only is that a breach of client confidentiality, the client who receives the new draft document with someone else's kids names or other information on it will a) think you do sloppy work (he'll be right), b) think you don't care much about his case, c) think you didn't spend as much time as you billed on his document and question your bill and d) wonder how carefully you protect *his* data.

---

2   More about this in Chapter 11 on Billing.

Checklists, outlines and other time saving tools

There's no excuse not to use them.

Develop a client intake sheet for potential clients to fill out in the waiting room before the first appointment. That way you aren't billing the client at your hourly rate to get an address, phone numbers, email and relevant contact info for the file. Instead, you're billing someone else for work done on another case while the new client completes the intake sheet.

Develop a standard client questionnaire and let the client fill it out at home. That way you're not burning billable hours asking about the basics. Your clients are on notice of the kind of information they need to start gathering and of the importance of their participation in the proceeding. You don't want to be chasing down bank account numbers at the last minute. The questionnaire can be augmented as needed and as additional information surfaces.

Always keep the questionnaire in the same place in the file for easy reference. Consider printing it on a different color of paper so you can find it quickly. I copied mine on green paper and told my clients that it was green for money, because the better and more complete the information they gave me, the less they would pay me to track it down myself.

If there is a series of procedures which you follow repeatedly (such as joining pensions, obtaining wage assignments, or similar processes), create a checklist so you can be sure nothing falls through the cracks. There are some good legal software packages out there which do this for you so long as you do the R & D to set them up properly at the beginning.

A checklist will let you quickly ascertain what discovery is outstanding, what pleadings need to be drafted, when they are due and the like. You can get a snapshot of the status of each case by turning to a single piece of paper which is always in the same place in your file, or in an easily accessible computer sub-file called "Pending" under each client's name. As you get busier, this will be a godsend. It's another way be sure you are on top of your case and avoids that horrible feeling just before the discovery cut off that you forgot to send out a key subpoena and it's too late now.

Always keep the partially filled out checklist in the same place (perhaps the inside cover of the file) so you or your staff can quickly reference it and know what discovery or other process is outstanding, when it is due, what is done and what needs to be done next. Train your staff to routinely check this list when they run out of work while you are at court. That way you are not paying for down time.

Fee agreements

Like the shoemaker's shoeless children, lawyers are often lousy at fee agreements. Make sure you have one signed by the client before you start working. Always put it in the same place in the file for easy reference. Don't let this one slip. I know you're so excited about having a case that you can't wait to get started on it. Invariably, the case where you forget to get the fee agreement signed is the one which results in a fee dispute.

Lawyers are even more lousy at keeping their fee agreements current. We take on a new case, tell our legal assistant to send out the standard fee letter, and never think about it. Do take the time to review and revise it periodically to be sure that it is current and clearly sets out the terms of the financial relationship you want to have with your clients. If it provides for replenishing the retainer in the trust account at particular periods, be sure you flag the client's billing records. A provision in your fee agreement requiring replenishment is no good to you if you forget to ask for it when the retainer is depleted.

Confidentiality

This is much more than not gossiping about your cases.

Consider using a number or code to identify client files. It's much harder for someone who sees you reading your file or referring to your to banker's box at court to figure out who you represent if you use a code, not a name. And files that are numerical rather than alphabetical are less likely to be misfiled. If you intend to represent the rich and famous, or just the locally well known, this is essential.

Think about where you put the outgoing mail in your office. I blew this one once. For the convenience of my staff, we collected outgoing mail in a basket near the front door which made it easy for the mail carrier to collect. I learned the error of my ways one day when the UPS delivery person had just delivered a package, and on his way out, spotted a well known professional athlete's name in the outgoing mail basket. He asked if I represented the person named (whose home address, I might add, was a closely guarded secret, but easily visible on my letter to him) and what I thought of his chances for next season. End of *that!* From that point forward, all outgoing mail or other correspondence with a client's name and address was collected at a very benign (and unobservable to the public) place. Better yet, have your staff routinely drop all outgoing correspondence personally in a nearby mailbox at the end of the day instead of leaving it for your carrier to collect when your mail is delivered.

This also applies to clients walking behind your assistant's desk (where pending work is spread out for all to see) or walking behind your own desk to look over your shoulder at the monitor as you run guideline support calculations. The best practice is to keep client work covered or put it away so no one else can inadvertently see it. A friend of mine who specializes in defending lawyers against State Bar complaints takes this very seriously. If you walk into his office, you won't see a single file anywhere. You won't even see a piece of paper other than a clean legal pad on his desk. And if a client wanders into your file room, or a part of the office where other clients' information is available, gently but firmly escort them out. It helps to explain to them that you take your duty of confidentiality very seriously and guard *their* legal information just as scrupulously.

Never talk to one client on the phone while another is within earshot in the waiting room. If your voice carries (and mine always did) close your office door.

If you are faxing or emailing documents to your client at work (I'm told there are some people who still use faxes), make sure you call him first so that he is standing by the fax machine when they come over. The last thing your client wants is for his confidential business to be sitting on the office fax machine for his coworkers to see. And don't forget that if he uses his work computer, his employer may own the content of his hard drive, including your confidential email communications. And if you're sending it to him at home, don't forget that the kids might see it. Again, make sure your client will be the first and only one to see any confidential material which you send. And if your client instructs you to go ahead and fax to a less than secure machine without calling first, make sure you have that instruction in writing in your file.

Sharing office space

I will it say again: you are always judged by the company you keep. Be careful with whom you are willing to share a reputation, especially as yours is being formed. It can take years to undo a bad reputation by association.

If you are on your own, it is often helpful to share office space with someone else. You can share the fixed expenses, such as rent, phone and the like. Perhaps you can share staff if you don't need someone full time. If they are busy, they may be willing to hand off overflow work to you. Sometimes they will allow you to work off part of your rent by doing legal work on their cases. This is not only good experience, but helps with the cash flow. After all, you're probably not that busy yet. And it always helps to have someone you can bounce ideas off of, especially while you are learning.

This can go wrong, however, if you aren't careful. If the person you are sharing space with is a crook, or just a jerk, you may be tarred by the association. And of course, since you'll be working in close proximity to them, if you aren't compatible, both in personality and work habits, you may make each other crazy.

There's a corollary to this. If you share space with a colleague against whom you'd love to have lots of cases, you've probably created a conflict, even if you lock your files in your personal office. How do you prevent his staff from overhearing your or your staff's conversations with your own client?

If you're going to share space, make it with someone whose reputation is complimentary to your own, but at the same time someone against whom you don't expect to have cases. That's why a lot of lawyers elect to share space with a lawyer in a different field of practice.

Know your limitations

If your mother makes you nuts, don't accept her clone as a client; the transference will make your life a living hell. (more about this under Finding and Screening Clients).

If you have a problem with deadlines, set up a system of early reminders, including multiple redundancies, and pay attention to them.

If you work best in the morning, do your most intense work then and save the afternoon for returning phone calls.

If you tend to be disorganized, find and use tools to help you: create detailed "to do" lists and scrupulously follow them. Use your phone as the asset it was designed to be. And, if this still isn't enough, hire a really tough legal assistant.

You'll really need to make to do lists, and update them daily. Not only is this good practice, there's an important psychology to it. It feels good to cross things off. It's also a reminder to be sure you billed for the time you spent when you are crossing something off the list. Most smart phones make this easy. If you use your phone, make sure you sync it with the office software so that your staff also sees the list and know the deadlines.

Phone Calls and Emails

Lawyers' failure to communicate is the number one source of client complaints. Return phone calls promptly; within 24 hours is a good rule of thumb. And if you can't talk to the client now, at least leave a message telling him when you will be able to. Remember, your clients are totally obsessed with their case, and are probably waiting by the phone to tell you about the latest crisis. Be sensitive, and let the client know you take their concerns seriously.

The same is true for email and texting, as most of us are relying ever more heavily on technology in our practices. Email has the beauty of being immediate. It also creates the expectation of an immediate response. The client who is sitting at his computer all day may have unrealistic expectations about how quickly you can get back to him with an answer to his question. Be very clear with clients about your expectations for email. Let them know that you are often in court, in depositions, conferring with other clients, or otherwise engaged in activities which take you away from your computer. Assure them that you will respond promptly when you can, and then do so. And as with telephone calls, never let it go more than 24 hours without a response.

Also, don't let the immediacy of email cause you send a reply which is less than thoughtful and carefully considered. It often takes time to work out the correct professional response.

How to paper your file

Right now, you probably remember every phone call and every detail of every case. Trust me: it will not always be thus. There will be too many clients and the cases will start to run together. You'll soon learn that the same issues and patterns come up over and over, in different guises with different names.

Make sure you have good information in your file where you can access it. The case is the most important thing going on your client's life right now, and he expects you to have all the details at your fingertips. He won't be happy if you have to keep asking the names and ages of his children or the length of the marriage. He especially won't like it if you keep describing him as an engineer and he's a geologist. I know an attorney who did this once, after he'd been in the case for over a year! The client was *not* happy.

Develop good work habits now, because you won't have time later as you get busier. In the old days before speech recognition software, I used to pick up the dictaphone and dictate a memo of every phone call before I either placed or took the next call. It didn't take long, and created a great record. It meant a lot of typing for my assistant, but my files were impeccable.

Speech recognition software is a less expensive way to do this, especially since the memos don't have to be pretty or perfect; they just have to record the content in a way that will either jog your memory or cover you in the fee arbitration.[3] This is particularly efficient if you have a headset with a top quality microphone, which switches from the phone to your computer.

If you're more comfortable with a keyboard, type the memo, but it may take you longer than it would to talk it into the computer microphone.

Include the time you took to dictate or type the memo in the charge for the phone call. It is part of the same service, and you should get paid for it.

Don't just put your chicken-scratched notes in the file. You may not be able to read them later, and if you are deposed on them (God forbid!) it's really easy for a good cross examiner to cast doubt. Save your notes, but supplement them with a legible memo

When appropriate, send a copy of the memo of a particularly important conversation, such as an interview with a key witness, to your client. It reminds him that you are working on his case even when he isn't there, and gives him a flavor of the information you are gathering on his behalf.

And it goes without saying that you shouldn't put negative editorial comments about your client or opposing counsel in your memo unless you are willing to have to explain them later to the person you maligned. The client owns the file, not you, and if they substitute you out, you are required to give them the original.[4] They won't like seeing that you thought they were a lying sack of something smelly.

---

3 See detailed discussion in How to Win a Fee Arbitration.

4 If you are substituted out, always keep a copy of the file for yourself. If it's electronic, that's easy. If it is paper, it is worth the cost of copying when they come back and say you didn't do something that you know you did do.

Note any follow up activity after a phone call, such as "Joe will fill out the financial disclosures and drop them by with copies of his pay stubs by Monday." Then put the financial disclosures on your follow up list for Monday.

When you return a phone call, note the date and time on the message slip and put it in the file. If you left a message, write "msg" or "voicemail" on the slip. If there was no answer, write "N/A" and save it by your phone to try again later. Save the message slip and after you've made contact, staple it to the memo of the call.[5]

As I've said before, develop good work habits now. You won't have time later, and it's always easier to learn than unlearn.

The ugly green monster on the corner of your desk

This is the case you don't want to deal with. Sometimes it's because you don't know what to do with it. Sometimes it's because you have to deliver bad news. Sometimes it's because you're afraid you've screwed it up (more on this later). Sometimes it's because you aren't getting paid to do it. Sometimes it's because the client makes you crazy.

Incidentally, if the reason you don't want to work on it is that you aren't getting paid, or the client is truly making you crazy, you probably should be developing a strategy to get out of the case (without abandoning the client, of course).

Problem cases are not fine wines and don't improve with age. The file will sit there, creating a mild sense of discomfort every time you look at it. If you have one of these, do yourself a favor: Force yourself to deal with it and then reward yourself for being such a good trooper.

Besides, it's almost never as bad as you thought it was going to be when you finally sit down and give it your attention. And if it is as bad (or worse)

---

5 This is a great practice for dealing with the client or opposing attorney who complains "you never return my calls" and you can quote date and time of each returned call, together with the fact that *they* didn't call *you* back.

than you thought, figure out how you got into this mess and how you can be sure to see another like it coming and avoid it in the future. If you really did screw up, damage control always gets harder with the passage of time. If it's a failure of follow up, seriously look at your tickler system and implement office systems to see that it never happens again.

Do the thing you hate most first, then reward yourself by doing something you really like, or going out for a quick latte. Besides, you'll enjoy it much more if the hard thing is done than if you're dreading the fact that it is still waiting for you back at the office.

Three

What is an advocate, anyway?

A good advocate gets the best possible result for her client, given the facts and law of the case. You can't turn the proverbial sow's ear into a silk purse, but you can do the best with what you've got.

That being said, you don't have to make *every* possible argument, no matter how attenuated, and you will probably be more effective if you don't. There was once a young lawyer who appeared before me. I knew she was very bright, but after making her legitimate arguments on behalf of her client, would launch into the weakest of long shots. As the judge, it irritated me tremendously. Then one day, just before launching into one of these, she said "I just wouldn't feel I was doing my job as an advocate if I didn't point out......" and I got it. She defined her job as an advocate as making every possible point, even the weakest. It didn't help her, but that was what she was taught. My approach was the opposite. List all potential arguments and then drop the weakest one. Those are for dire emergencies only, *not* standard advocacy.

And it goes without saying that just because your client wants you to say it doesn't mean it should be said. Remember, the client is renting your brain for a purpose and if the argument he wants you to make will hurt the case rather than help it, you must point that out to your client, even if he really, really, really wants to hear you say it. And then, sometimes there are things the client absolutely has to hear you say. There are ways to do it so that you don't lose credibility with the judge: "Your Honor, my client feels strongly that…" makes the point without causing the judge to think that you, too, think the stupid argument is persuasive. Another way to convey this message is to say "Your Honor, as an advocate, I am compelled to point out that…" Use these sparingly. Remember, if your job is just to parrot whatever the client wants, why did you go to law school and develop your professional training? He might as well hire his cousin or the guy on the corner to speak for him.

Good advocacy is a lot more than learning how to "huff and puff and blow their house down."

Why it is important to develop a case plan and how to do it

If you don't know where you are going, how will you know how to get there, much less when you have arrived?

A case plan helps you spot the weaknesses in your case or evidence early when there is more time to fix them. It helps you determine what kind of litigation budget your client needs to allow for. And if the client's litigation budget is insufficient, you can consult with him early to limit your involvement to what is most important to him rather than waiting until you've done all the work for which he can't pay. This is also the time to determine whether limited scope representation may be a good option for your client.[6]

It's easy to do a case plan on a computer. Put your word processor in outline mode and start with a list of the issues you know about (more will come up later). Under each issue, briefly list the information you will need to make your case. Under the information needed, note whether you can

6 See my book *Unbundling Your Divorce: How to Find a Lawyer to Help You Help Yourself,* available at amazon.com.

get it from your client, the other party, or through subpoena or deposition. List any witnesses you think you might need to interview or depose. List any possible issues on which you might need an expert witness. It isn't a bad idea to add a timetable for locating your expert (and remember, they need lead time) as well as some possible names. If possible, list a target date on which you want to send things out, and add that to your tickler system.

Figure out what you need to do first and start doing it, crossing things off the list as you go. If the information you get leads to additional questions or information you need (and it usually will), add those to the list.

Update the plan periodically as you get the information or more issues arise, and put the revision date and time stamp in an automatically updated footer at the bottom of the page so you always know you are working from the most recent version.

This is a great way to give your client homework assignments. It keeps them busy, so they call you less often for a progress report. It lets them feel (correctly) that they are participating in their case. Best of all, it lets you concentrate on the things you went to law school for instead of chasing down bank or retirement plan statements. Your client spends his legal dollar on useful legal work rather than on things he could do for himself. That means you're less likely to find yourself in fee arbitration.

It's also great for the days when business is slow and you run out of work. Just pick up the case plan, look at what hasn't been done, figure out the next step and draft the subpoena, write the letter, or whatever. Instruct your staff to periodically check the case plan, and remind you of things coming up so they can be worked into the normal workload. If it's something your paralegal can do, even better. Then, when you're in court and he's looking for work, he knows exactly where to look for it and you're not paying for wasted time until you can get back from court and give further instructions.[7]

---

7 And if you've done everything you have to do, and still have no work, go sit in the back of a busy courtroom and watch how other people do it. If you're not billing, you might as well be learning.

Even in my biggest cases, I liked to keep a little file called "To Do" with the most recent version of the case plan, any current checklists, and the time-table of current deadlines. It was always right in front where it was most accessible.

Personal research files

As appellate decisions come out, or you do research on an issue that is new to you, set up a research file organized by subject matter. These can be physical files where you put a hard copy, or a folder on your computer where you save links to key cases and articles. When you are starting out, they may be basic things like child support or wage assignments. As you write a killer brief on stock options, throw an extra copy in the stock options research file. Do the same with prenuptial, settlement or other agreements. Keep a file on business valuation experts, real estate appraisers, custody evaluators and counselors. When a good business valuation report or custody report comes across your desk, put an extra copy in your reference files. It will help you prepare your deposition or cross examination of the next expert witness you face if you have an idea of what should be in a good report and what might be missing from theirs. That way, you start collecting a library of forms and reports, research and resources. Otherwise, you will be racking your brain to remember the name of the case where you filed the research, only to realize that the file is in off-site storage.

Weaknesses??? WHAT weaknesses?

Always look for the holes in your own case. Otherwise, how can you fix or minimize them? Too many lawyers assume the validity of their client's ver-sion of the facts without discrimination. This isn't to say that all your clients will lie to you, but they *will* put the best spin on their story, and of course, they are not objective. It isn't a pleasant experience to get blindsided at court because you took your client's story at face value and didn't realize it doesn't bear scrutiny. You won't enhance either their case or your professional reputation if you forget this rule.

The case plan is a good place to start looking for the weaknesses.

Of course, your opposing counsel will be only too happy to point more of them out to you when you have your first phone conversation or meeting.

By the way, just because your case has weaknesses, and you can't figure out a way to fix them, don't concede them all. Remember to keep something in your back pocket to concede in settlement negotiations. Also, the judge is never going to give you everything you ask for, so make sure you have a couple of throw away issues you don't mind losing (as long as they aren't totally stupid and indefensible: that impairs your credibility).

The importance of being consistently professional

Family lawyers are unique in the bar in that most of us represent both husbands and wives. As a result, we have to be able to argue both sides of every issue.

Clients will sometimes want you to take a position that you don't feel comfortable with. Sometimes it is because they think that is what the law *ought* to be, even though you've told them that's not the way it *is*. Never take a stupid position just because your client wants you to. Remember, you're building your professional reputation every time you interact with a colleague or a judge. It's *your* reputation on the line, not your client's. If you violate this rule and allow your professional credibility to be undermined, you and your future clients will be paying for it for years.

When I would tell a client the position he wanted me to take on his behalf was directly contrary to the law, and he said I should "try it anyway, because the worst they can say is no" my answer was always the same: "Presumably the reason you came to me was because of my reputation with the courts. That was developed over years of appearing before judges and letting them know that I know my craft and don't make untenable arguments. I'm not going to blow that reputation for myself and my future clients for any one case, even yours." If they insist, they need to find another lawyer.

Distinguishing a gripe from a legal issue

We always want to be able to solve the client's problem. However, there isn't a legal redress for every "wrong." This is especially true for all the perceived wrongs in an intimate relationship that has gone sour. You can't fix everything. When you tell a client the bad news, some of them will imply that you *could* if you were a really good lawyer. Don't fall into this trap, and don't let them make you feel there's something wrong with you if you can't save them from the consequences of all the stupid decisions they've made in the past.

Your job is to deal with the legal issues. Not all problems lend themselves to legal solutions. If she married a jerk, you can't change the jerk into the guy she thought he was when she married him, or the one she wishes she'd married instead. As a lawyer you take the facts and the personalities as you find them.

If what they really want is a personality transplant for a spouse, there are ways to remind the client that it was his choice:

"I'm sure you wish you had chosen a different parent for your children."

"I'm sure you never saw this side of him/her before you married."[8]

Your job is to resolve your clients' legal problems to the best of your ability, not to give them a "do over" on life or become a guarantor for their own poor choices.

---

8 I said this to a lot of clients, and in 25 years, only one was honest enough to say "Oh, I saw it all right; I just never thought he'd turn it on *me*."

How many cases at a time is enough?

Never take on more cases than you can realistically handle. Most family lawyers blow this one. They let accounts receivable get out of hand, then need to take on more cases to get the retainers to cover cash flow while they are waiting to get paid on the old cases. The problem is that when they do this, they have compounded the problem. After the new retainer is exhausted, they have *another* case on which they are waiting to get paid, and so they take on more new cases to get *that* retainer, and on and on. Pretty soon they're in so deep they can't get out. Then they start stacking the files around their office and complaining that they are so busy they haven't been able to take a vacation in two years. In the meantime, their unhappy clients are complaining to their friends that they can't get their case finished, or can't get in to see their lawyer, and their friends are going somewhere else for representation. As I've said elsewhere, represent people competently and efficiently, and they will send their friends to you. And then do the same for their friends.

If you've got a stack of unfinished projects on your desk, that's probably a good sign that you need to get your current workload under control before you take on more. And there's no harm in telling a client that you are "too busy" to take their case. They'll probably want you even more because they interpret that as a sign that you're good at what you do and may be willing to wait. If they don't, that's ok, too. There are always more clients if you do a good job, and the best source of client referrals is always word of mouth from other satisfied clients. They won't be satisfied clients (and thus good referral sources) if you are so busy signing up new retainers that you can't finish their case.

Violation of this rule is a guarantee of unhappy clients, sloppily prepared documents, poor work, a weak professional reputation, and impaired quality of life. And remember, the *best* thing you can hope for from unhappy clients is no future referrals and a bill that is paid in full; the worst is a fee arbitration, malpractice claim, or a complaint to the State Bar.

Expert witnesses

When you're new, try to use the best experts in the field. They know how to do it right and you can learn a great deal from them. Later on, after *you* know how to do it right, you can expand and try out other experts. If you do it the other way around, you won't know when your own expert screws up (and they do).

Remember, you are still responsible for your expert's work. You're the one who is going to be sued if it goes sour, and it's no defense to say "I relied on my expert." *You* picked the expert, the client didn't. And by the way, *never* let the client pick the experts.

Learn almost as much as your expert knows

Even experts make mistakes. If you don't know finance, how will you effectively depose a financial expert?

Learn how to read a tax return, a balance sheet, a profit and loss statement, and how to spot red flags which need expert assistance. Learn about deferred compensation, stock options, business valuations, and any other issues which are likely to arise in your cases.

Learn the difference between cash and accrual accounting and why that alone can significantly skew a balance sheet and manipulate the bottom line.

The Expert "Lawyer Wannabe"

Never let the expert run your case. Lots of experts are attracted to forensic work because they're lawyer wannabes. Frequently that's what makes them so good at it. It doesn't mean they are bad experts, just that they aren't lawyers. Some experts like to script their own questions. This can be helpful if you are just starting out and don't know much about the field. But don't forget that you are the lawyer, and the one ultimately responsible.

You need to know when to rein your experts in. Don't let them take extreme positions which can't be defended (it's amazing how many will try). I used an expert for years who did great work for me, and whom I took apart on the witness stand when he was hired by the other side. One opposing counsel asked me "How come you always win with him and I always get creamed when I use him against you?" The only variable was that when he worked for me, I didn't allow him to take extreme positions which made him vulnerable under cross examination. Other attorneys let him run the case and he was a much less effective witness for them.

Read your own expert's report as critically as though you are cross examining her yourself. Make sure you understand it thoroughly, and make her explain anything you don't understand. If you don't get it, you can't effectively present it, or defend against your opponent's cross examination. You are ultimately the one responsible for your expert's work, since you're the one who will get sued if she screws up.

Protecting your experts

If you want the good experts to work on your cases, make sure that you give them all the information they need to do their job effectively at the earliest possible time. That way they can work it into their regular schedule. If you always give them the info at the last minute, you'll either get sloppy work, no report, or an expert who refuses to work with you in the future. They all have black lists and you don't want to be on it.

The same rule about taking on too much work applies to experts as well. Like many attorneys, they may accept too many cases, and then fall behind on their workload. Make sure that you and your expert are on the same page as to the work to be done and the completion time.

And make sure they get paid, or they won't work with you again.

Taking depositions

Taking a good deposition can be harder than putting on a trial. Presumably at trial, you know what the answer to your question is going to be before you ask it. At deposition, you may not have a clue. Also, at trial you have a chance to regroup and catch your breath a bit while your opponent is putting on his case. When taking the deposition, you're on stage the whole time.

Have a good outline of the topics you want to cover and be prepared to depart from it if necessary. If a new lead comes up, and it is likely to, the most effective tactic is to follow it to its conclusion immediately. That means you have to be able to depart from your outline, then return to it without losing your place or your concentration. This is a skill you simply must learn, and it is equally important when testimony takes an unexpected turn in court. You'll either forget to follow up on the new lead, which gives your witness time to figure out that he made a mistake and what to do about it, or you'll lose your place in your original line of questioning. Either can be a disaster. And if you're fumbling around, your client won't be impressed.

Prepare for a deposition as if you are preparing for trial, because that's exactly what you are doing. Lots of mediocre lawyers wing depositions, especially after they've gotten a bit of experience under their belt. Don't. Get all the information you can as succinctly as possible. You're not paid by the word (though the court reporter is) and there's no gold star for expanding three hours of information into a nine hour deposition. Your client will assume you're churning fees. Opposing counsel will assume you are either churning or don't know what you are looking for.

Never just run a hostile deposition witness through their trial testimony. Depositions are about getting information. They aren't a dress rehearsal for trial, and you're nuts if you give the witness a roadmap of where you intend to go by simply running through your trial questions. If you do, you will have handed the witness several weeks (or months) to figure out how to perform more effectively by the time trial rolls around and they do it again in front of the judge. They will also have a transcript of the deposition to refer to. That guarantees they have time to figure out where they messed up so they do it better when the judge is listening. This is a common new lawyer mistake.

Never grandstand in a deposition; there's no one in a black robe watching and giving style points.

Never play all your cards in a deposition. That's not what it is for. Save something for trial, and never argue with the witness.

And here's an obvious one. If your client is being deposed and you need to take a break to talk to him, don't do it in front of the other attorney's staff. Your client's deposition will likely be taken in the opposing attorney's office. The staff can hear everything you say, and guess whose side they are on? I had an extremely experienced attorney do this in my office. His client wasn't doing well in the deposition, so they asked for a break. Right in front of my legal assistant, the attorney told the client what he was doing wrong, and coached him on how to lie. Talk about treating staff like the furniture! Under the pretext of checking to see if we needed any more water or coffee, my assistant dropped me a note telling me exactly what was going on, an I was able to ask the witness what instructions he had just been publicly given. Remember, there's no expectation of privacy when a lawyer talks to his client in front of other people. Not only should you not treat your own staff like potted plants, you shouldn't treat the other guy's staff that way either.

Preparing your client for his deposition and testimony

Always prepare your client to testify, but never script answers for him. He'll sound like a lawyer wrote them, and any savvy lawyer or judge will know the difference. Your client's credibility will suffer. Tell him what facts are important, but let him put them in his own words.

Also, do them the courtesy of giving them time to prepare themselves. Don't wait until the day before the deposition to prepare your client, or there won't be time to fill in any holes in the evidence or their testimony. I always found three days before the deposition to be the optimum amount of lead time. It wasn't so far in advance that they forgot what I told them, and not so close to showtime that they didn't have time to let it jell.

If you are preparing your client for court rather than deposition, you have to do both sides, direct and cross examination.

After you've prepared him for his own testimony, do a dry run of cross examination, pretending you're the opposing counsel. It is even a good idea to take a physical break. Tell him you are going to walk out the door, and when you come back, you are Attorney X (who will be cross examining him). This is helpful on a number of levels. It is one thing to tell your story to a sympathetic advocate who is in your corner. It is another to tell it to someone who is hostile, and who is doing their best to poke holes in it. Not only is this a good way for him to see how cross examination works, it's good practice for you. It's also a reality check for him and helps point out the weaknesses of his own testimony. Many litigants are highly resistant to the suggestion that there are any weaknesses in their case. After they have had to endure your cross examination, they may be more realistic. Also, most people are scared to death to be put on the spot and will be grateful for the thoroughness with which you prepare them.

When to line up your witnesses

Early and often. Confirm all dates and deadlines in writing. The good expert witnesses are very busy. They have calendar conflicts, too, and are entitled to be treated with courtesy. There's no excuse for using a less able expert witness on an issue because you didn't think your case through early enough to line up a more effective one.

Remember, too, that just because the client says "I've got lots of witnesses" and proceeds to tell you exactly what Uncle Joe will say, when you finally talk to Uncle Joe (the night before trial) you may get an entirely different story. Big mistake.

When you talk to potential witnesses, don't forget to ask the questions your opponent will be asking. You may be surprised by the answers. Better that you are surprised in the interview than at trial.

Oops! Tomorrow's the settlement conference

Always learn your case *before* the settlement conference. Too many lawyers don't, and they miss important opportunities. Know what your client's best and worst case results are, and discuss the range with her before the settlement conference. Otherwise, how will you recognize a favorable settlement offer when you see it, make a good offer yourself, and how will you properly advise your clients on the benefits and risks of accepting or countering it?

This also gives you a huge advantage over your opponents, many of whom won't have focused on their case yet because they are still putting out fires and taking more cases than they can handle to get the retainers in the trust account.

Never underestimate your opponent

You may *know* you've prepared your case until you can recite it in your sleep. You know your opponent hasn't even met with his client to start preparing because his client is complaining to your client that she can't get in to see her attorney, though she's been trying for weeks.[9] Don't get complacent. Don't underestimate him. He's been doing it a lot longer than you have. And there are a few lawyers out there who have a gift for dancing rings around their opponents because they are just that good on the balls of their feet.

This came up with a young lawyer who once worked for me. He had a hearing against an attorney who was notorious for taking five different cases on a morning calendar, and spending all of ten minutes on the morning of the hearing to prepare. My associate was a good and careful lawyer, who had learned just enough to get a little cocky. He stopped by my office one day to chortle a bit about how unprepared his opponent was going to be for tomorrow's hearing. I told him to go back to his office and go over his notes again to be sure nothing had been omitted. The next day, a much chastened young

---

9   And this is a good reminder that in family law, opposing parties talk to each other all the time, complain about their attorneys, discuss trial strategy, quote what you said about the opposing counsel and generally undercut you. Don't be the one whose client is complaining to the other side.

attorney trailed into my office on returning from court. He had done well, but his "unprepared" opponent had given him a real run for his money. Years later when I ran into my former associate at court, he reminded me of that hearing and said he'd never forgotten the lesson. When you are learning, prepare, and then prepare again, even if on your own time.

The difference between "real" time and "lawyer" time

Learn to give accurate time estimates and stay within them. Violation of this rule is a primary pet peeve of judges. If your opponent drones on and on, the judge will know who is trying a crisp case and who isn't. I learned this from an old time lawyer. I couldn't figure out why his cases always got called first and everyone else's had to wait. I accused him (with my usual tact in those days) of being a favorite with the judge. He told me to clock his time estimate. The judges knew they could take his estimates to the bank and wouldn't risk a mistrial. If the judge has several cases to be heard and only time for one, she's likely to give the time to the lawyer she knows will conclude on time and not run over.

Cross examination isn't a refresher course

Don't use cross examination to run a witness through their direct testimony a second time. This is a beginner giveaway. All you're doing is making sure the judge hears the damaging testimony twice. You're likely to burn your trial time and irritate the judge to boot.

The effective cross examiner exposes the weaknesses in the direct testimony, lets the judge draw the inference that the testimony is suspect, and then shuts up and sits down. Don't just keep hammering on the obvious: "You don't *really* know, do you? Do you? Do you?"

Even if the witness you are cross examining is a lying sack of camel dung, always treat them courteously. Calling them "sir" (and not sarcastically, of course) is an extremely effective technique and underscores your own professionalism.

How to ask a question and other no-brainers they don't teach you in law school

Sad to say, many lawyers, even experienced ones, ask lousy questions. Learn to ask clear, concise questions. Avoid compound and complex ones. There's no excuse to not master the nuts and bolts of trial practice. Learn how to ask tight questions. Don't just make a declarative statement followed by "isn't that true?" or worse, "right?" That is a technique which you should use sparingly in cross examination to use the witnesses own words against him. Instead, ask short, simple declarative questions.

Don't use cross examination to argue the law or to argue with the witness. Testimony is about facts and law is law. Arguing with a witness is only marginally less damaging than arguing with the judge.

Don't keep asking the same question over and over hoping to get a different answer. You won't.

Learn the rules of evidence. Most of your opponents will be lousy at this, and you'll shine if you have mastered them.

Speaking of rules, learn the local rules of court like the back of your hand, and use them. Volunteer to serve on the rules committee if you get the opportunity; you'll learn loads. Ditto any written Local Practice Guides.

Learn to spot evasive or ambiguous answers and follow up on the spot. If you have to stick to a script, you'll lose the chance to present an integrated, cohesive case. Worse, you may not remember to come back and point out the ambiguity, or if you do, the judge may have forgotten why it is important. As with depositions, it is important to thoroughly outline your questions so you know how to get where you want to go. Equally importantly, you have to be able to depart from your outline to follow up on a new line of questioning on the spot, and be able to pick up where you left off. This is just good lawyering.

These are the tools of your trade, folks. It isn't that hard, but few people make the effort to truly master them. Do yourself and your clients a favor and be one of the exceptions.

I just got out of law school. Why do I have to do CLE?

There are lots of good reasons, starting with the fact that many law schools tend to focus either on pure academics or training you to pass the bar. Neither of these has much to do with the actual practice of law. And if you went to one of those law schools where the curriculum is driven by the school's national ranking, your school may well have had the attitude that clinical (i.e. real life hands-on how to do it) programs are somehow beneath them. As a result, you may not have much practical knowledge of how it is done in the real world. Always take all continuing education classes appropriate to your specialty and level of knowledge. Even if you know the basic law, you'll learn a lot of nuance. And many law schools teach from old case law because it illustrates an issue. That may or may not leave you qualified to answer the question of the current law in a changing field. And family law is nothing if not a constantly changing field.

There's another reason to do it. These programs not only provide an opportunity to learn your craft; you'll also be meeting colleagues with whom you can compare experiences. You might even meet that mentor you've been looking for. And of course, they'll learn that you are out there and they might just send you some smaller cases to see how you do.

Make a special effort to take classes called "Accounting for Lawyers," "How to Read a Tax Return," or "Finance for Lawyers." These are tailored to the kinds of information lawyers need, and all too many of our colleagues don't take advantage of them. If you know more accounting or finance than your opponent, you'll do rings around him (and maybe even his expert, by the way). If your local society of forensic CPAs offers a course on tax or accounting just for divorce lawyers, don't miss it. You will not only get an opportunity to meet the top divorce forensics in your area, they can teach you where to look for the weaknesses in your opposing CPA's report (or, indeed, your own expert's). These people aren't trying to teach you to be an accountant, but they can be invaluable in teaching you how to be a better lawyer when dealing with tax and accounting issues.

How to know when you're out of your depth and what to do about it

One of the attorneys I respect most is someone who knows when a case is out of his league and isn't so ego-involved or financially desperate that he tries to keep it anyway. Now, when you are starting out, everything will seem to fall into this category. You may be spending a lot of your own time educating yourself on the subject/issues/law/procedures. That's how you learn. It isn't right to bill the client for the learning curve, so you'll be doing a lot of this on your own time.

If that isn't enough, seek out an experienced colleague who might be able to give you some pointers. In an appropriate case, it may be a good idea to actually buy an hour of his time. Most lawyers are willing to help bright young attorneys, and if you have developed a rapport with one, that can be a real life saver when you find yourself over your head.

Another good approach is to join (or create) a study group of other lawyers at a similar level of practice. Study groups are a fixture of law school, and can be immensely helpful in practice. Of course, since you will be talking about the specifics of cases, they have to be professionals whom you can trust, and you have to be careful of disclosing confidential information. That being said, it can be a great benefit to pose a problem and see what ideas others may have about resolving it.

If the case is really beyond your present ability to handle, consider associating in a more experienced attorney to assist. If you don't and decide to take it on, knowing you aren't qualified to do it, and without taking steps to fill in the gaps in your knowledge, you may be committing a breach of ethics, or even malpractice.

Four

C lients are the heart and soul of your practice. Without them, you'd be waiting tables. So the intricacies of finding, keeping and firing clients are essential skills you simply must master if you are to be successful.

What kind of clients do you want, anyway?

Do you like custody cases, or do they make your stomach churn?

How do you feel about wading through eight inches of financial documents? If you hate it, don't take a big paper case, or make sure you have someone you can rely on do to the wading for you.

At the start, you are presumably handling a variety of matters. After all, when you're just starting out, your practice is going to be defined by the legal problems of the people who happen to consult you. Make note of the issues you enjoy working on and do well with (they are almost always the same) and which ones you tend to let slide because you don't like them. When I was a new lawyer, my law firm wanted me to do family law exclusively. Although I liked family law, I was determined to avoid the traditional gender stereotypes

44

which followed women in that era, where women lawyers were largely relegated to family law and probate. Because I wanted to avoid what I perceived to be a limiting stereotype, and because credibility in an entirely male and very old fashioned law firm was important to me, I fought my boss hard for a practice which was half real estate and half family law. What I found was that the real estate cases got done last because I enjoyed the family law cases more, and they moved at a faster pace. I realized that if I continued, something in the real estate cases would slip through the cracks, because family law was always a higher priority to me. Within a few months, I handed off the real estate cases to another associate and my practice was 100% family law. I'm glad I went through the exercise, though. When I limited my practice to family law, I knew it was my choice because that was what I preferred, and not because some male lawyer had pigeonholed me because I had ovaries and the other associates didn't.

Sometimes it isn't a particular area of practice, but a type of client that makes a difference. Make note of the clients you like or dislike. Look for patterns. Can you put your finger on something specific that made them either appealing or unappealing? These patterns repeat themselves, and by becoming aware of them, you can exercise better judgment in client selection if you are aware of the ones you like best. And since we always do better on projects we like than on those we loathe, you're more likely to develop good referral sources if you follow this advice. Remember, satisfied clients will talk about their case with their friends. That's how you build your practice.

Perhaps your dad is an engineer, so you speak engineer well. Personality types tend to be drawn to specific professions. Maybe you connect well with nurses, or first responders, or tech types. A colleague of mine represented a deputy sheriff in his first year in practice. Some years later, he figured out that he had represented more than half of the members of the department who had gotten a divorce or needed help with a custody or support issue. For some reason, I got along well with airline pilots and real estate contractors and before long there was a steady stream of them marching through my office.

Building referral sources

Referral sources start with people you already know: friends, acquaintances, neighbors, and the like. One great way to build referral sources is to get involved in your community. Don't join just to be joining. If you don't sincerely believe in the goals of the organization, the other members will sniff that out in a heartbeat. Find a local cause, group, or issue that interests you, and get involved. Volunteer for projects. After all, you are new and your dance card isn't full yet. Make sure you do a good job on any project you take on. People will be judging your competence and commitment and assume that good work habits and reliability as a volunteer translate into good work habits and responsibility to your clients. Not only is volunteering good for business because it expands the pool of people who know you are around; it is also the right way to live.

Also, not all new lawyers are young, having come to the law as a second career. If you fit that category, you have a ready-made referral source in your prior career. You have contacts, skills, and a reputation. These are all assets which can be used in building your law practice, as those people get divorced, have custody or support issues, and will be drawn to someone they already know and who speaks their language.

Other lawyers

I've already alluded to the importance of cultivating more experienced lawyers who represent the kind of clients you would like to have. The really good lawyers have so many potential clients that they can afford to be very selective. If they like you and think you're good, they may start sending their smaller referrals to you. If they do, send them a thank you note. I learned a particularly gracious way to do this from an old timer. He had designed a note card expressing his thanks for the referring lawyer's confidence in making the referral, and containing the assurance that he would do his utmost to assist the client if he was retained. He left a blank for the name of the client. When consulted by the potential new client, he would fill in the name and drop the card in the mail to the referring attorney. In the old days I had these professionally printed. Now you can do it on your own computer. Be sure to use good quality card stock. Fill in the client's name in longhand and, if you know the referring attorney well enough, write a brief personal thank you as well. Send it out promptly, and do it personally. This isn't something you have your office staff do, and it is an excellent business development tool. Another good tool, though it takes more time, is to personally dictate a letter to the referring attorney, thanking them for their confidence in you and assuring them that you will do your best for the client. It doesn't take long, makes a good impression, and is just plain good manners.

Other marketing tools

All law practices must be marketed in some way if they are to be successful. If you are part of a firm, they may take care of marketing. That's not an excuse for not promoting yourself. Join your local lawyer referral service panel. They are there for the purpose of matching lawyers and prospective clients. Take advantage of them.

Look closely at the kinds of clients you want to target. If they tend to be computer savvy, a good website is essential. Have it professionally designed. If you do it yourself, it will show. It doesn't cost that much, and the professional touch makes all the difference. In fact, websites are not only more flexible than other more traditional kinds of advertising, they are much cheaper to maintain.

Don't just use one of those canned lawyer formats with trite gavel and scales of justice clip art and fill in the blanks. Your website should be professional, but it should reflect *you*. Include your specialties and personal interests. It is helpful to have a Q & A or FAQ page to which prospective clients can refer. If there is a specific area of the law you prefer, target that. Include a mission statement saying why you were drawn to this field of law. Include information about your background and family. Family law clients like to know a little bit about their lawyer as a person. That being said, don't put your home address or phone number in any information going out to the public.

Include a professional portrait. Don't make the mistake one young woman lawyer I know did. She was so anxious to overcompensate for the fact that she is young that the picture she chose was, to use a gentle word, stern in the extreme. Frankly, if I didn't know her, that picture would have scared me to death. I'm sure she wanted to project the fact that she could be aggressive in protecting her clients' interests. I found it off-putting.

One good technique is to include a "Resources" page on your website, listing websites, books, and other helpful resources. It shows potential clients that you take their problems seriously and have gone to the trouble of investigating those resources which will help them have a more positive experience. Of course, you do need to carefully screen the resources you recommend yourself, in case you have inadvertently referred them to a lunatic fringe site with an appealing name.

And of course, always put your website on your business card, telephone ad or other promotional material.

Some client populations aren't particularly web-savvy. If your target client is relatively uneducated, they may rely heavily on yellow pages ads. I'm not a huge fan of these for general marketing, but there are client groups who can't be reached in large numbers any other way. As with the web, if you are going to go to the trouble and expense of a yellow pages ad (and they can be *very* expensive) do get some professional help on the design.

Many lawyers find brochures helpful, depending on the type of client they are targeting. They should be simple, eye-catching and professional. Think carefully about the kind of client you want to target and what they are most likely to respond favorably to. Don't print the brochure on cheap paper. Go to the expense of getting some professional brochure stock, or heavy weight paper in a pleasing, neutral color. Keep a stack of them in your waiting room, along with a stack of your business cards in an attractive display stand.

If you are bilingual, feature this *prominently* in all of your promotional literature. This is an important fact which sets you apart from the crowd. Don't assume that because your second language is French, and there isn't a large French-speaking local population, that it isn't important. Some referral sources will be looking solely for someone proficient in another language, and you want them to be able to find you. It's a good idea to invest in translating your promotional material into your second language. With the increasing cultural diversity of our country, it is important to remember that immigrants have important legal needs. The benefit to clients who are not fluent in English is obvious. However, even if they are English proficient, human nature being what it is, they will feel more comfortable dealing with someone with whom they feel a common cultural or linguistic bond.

Consider joining an ethnic bar association, (in *addition* to and not in lieu of the mainstream local bar, of course) if appropriate. You'll find other lawyers with whom you are culturally compatible, and cement ties into an ethnic community which can be a significant conduit for new clients.

Bone up on a recent law change or case which is relevant to the groups of clients you have targeted, and volunteer to speak at community centers, service organization meetings, or other groups where they are likely to be found. These organizations are always looking for qualified speakers. Similarly, consider crossover issues which other lawyers may not be targeting, such as the interplay between family law and immigration or bankruptcy issues, or some other topic of general interest to your target client base, and prepare a 30 to 45 minute talk on the subject.

Always hand out your business card and brochure (if you have one) at these functions.

The blind date: client screening and the initial interview

Client screening is an essential skill to develop. At the beginning, you may be so thrilled to have a client at all, that you will be gladly accepting people you would reject in a heartbeat if your dance card were not so empty. And, you are learning as you go. Not only are you learning your profession, but you are learning what kinds of clients you like and which ones you'd rather not deal with. How do you amass this information if you don't represent different types of people with varied legal problems?

I think it is a good idea to screen new clients yourself by phone before making an appointment (unless you have a *really* good and experienced legal assistant to do this for you.) When I was a new lawyer, the firm I worked for had a policy that every potential client who called got an appointment. The attorneys didn't make appointments, and new clients were never screened, except as to general subject matter, so that a family law case didn't go to a personal injury lawyer. I wouldn't have a clue what my 4:00 consultation was about except that it was somehow related to family law. This was a problem. I didn't know much yet, and would sometimes fumble around for an answer to their question. That didn't do much for the confidence of either of us. It would have been much better if I had had *some* idea what it was about so I could do some quick research in advance if I needed to instead of looking like a fool. It is a much better practice to talk to potential clients yourself than to just have your legal assistant make all appointments, and, by the way, don't charge for the five or ten minutes or so of the screening call.

Failure to screen potential clients was also a waste of time. There were any number of times when I would know within five minutes after the client walked in the door that this was not a case I was going to take. Nevertheless, courtesy demanded that I spend at least a half an hour letting them tell me their story. I couldn't charge them for the time because I knew I was going to send them away. It would have been far better if I had screened them first and, if I knew the case wasn't for me, referred them on, rather than wasting their time and my own.

Be prompt for all appointments. *You* hate waiting in your doctor's office; give your clients the same courtesy.

It is a good rule to reschedule client appointments only if it is unavoidable, such as when you are called to court for an emergency hearing. If it is the first appointment with a potential new client, the definition of unavoidable is that you were hit by a truck walking to your office. Their case is the most important thing happening in their lives. They've probably been on pins and needles since they made the appointment to see you. When you reschedule, it sends the message that their problem isn't very important to you. New lawyers often aren't very busy. Sometimes they want to *seem* busy because they think this will make the client think they're very, very good. What it will convey instead is that they are very, very rude. The initial interview is critical, and sets the tone for the rest of your interactions. You never get a second chance to do it right. Be courteous, professional and on time.

Limit the legalese. Don't be condescending or talk down to clients. Treat them with respect and insist that they treat you and your staff respectfully. I talk about staff in another section, and it is just good business to always treat your staff courteously whether or not anyone else is present. However, it is critically important in front of clients. I've seen people fire lawyers because of how they treated their staff. One client told me that after seeing how the first lawyer she consulted treated a staff person, she concluded he had no respect for women, and took her very lucrative case elsewhere (to me).

Be very clear about your billing arrangements and expectations. Some people find it difficult to talk about money. This is a business, and you simply must be able to clearly discuss your billing arrangements with clients.

Do a thorough intake interview. There are often critical facts that the client doesn't realize are important when they begin to tell you their story. It is your responsibility to ask the right questions.

Why it's sometimes a good thing to tell a client your strengths and weaknesses (after you've figured out what they are)

This helps set the ground rules for the relationship.

"I'm good at strategy and a poor hand holder. You are much better off using your therapist for that."

51

"I'm really good at getting down to the bottom line quickly, and impatient with delay."

"I'm very well organized and I hate doing things at the last minute, so I'll expect you to get me the information I ask for promptly."

I once had a client who had classic obsessive-compulsive disorder (OCD). As a result, she was extremely and uncontrollably anxious, and told me at the first meeting that due to her condition, she knew she would have to repeat things to me several times in order to be comfortable that she hadn't left something out. She would also need me to repeat information to her in order to reach a comfort level. This wasn't about money; she was willing to pay me for the time required and knew she needed the repetition to manage her anxiety. When I told her that I am impatient by nature, and not good at hand holding or repetition, it looked like our professional relationship was doomed at the start. Instead, we worked out an arrangement we could both live with. She needed lots of time to explain things and go over them more than once, and needed me to do the same.

The accommodation we reached was that if it was an emergency, I would do my best to be patient and allow her to take all the time that she needed. If it wasn't an emergency, she had free access to my legal assistant, whom she trusted and who was a wonderful listener. She could then make an appointment for a conference with me, for which I would set aside the time she would need to go over it all with me to her satisfaction, and I promised not to get impatient with her if it took a long time. We both agreed not to abuse this arrangement and it worked fine. She would call, tell my assistant what she needed to convey, and set up a time to talk to me in the next few days. I would find time in my schedule when I could give her my undivided attention, and even if the call went much longer than I would have liked, I promised to curb my impatience at her repetition.

This significantly reduced her anxiety for two reasons. First, she could focus on a specific time in the near future when she would have the time with me she needed. She also knew if she followed these ground rules, I wouldn't become impatient with her, so she was less anxious about upsetting me. The result was that we had an excellent working relationship on a very difficult and complex case, under circumstances which would otherwise have been disastrous. Had we not reached this accommodation early, I guarantee that she would have responded to my impatience at her repetition by feeling I was inattentive to her. I would have been irritated at having to repeat myself or watch the clock tick away for forty minutes on a phone call I thought should have taken fifteen. We couldn't have achieved the result we did without having set the ground rules first. After it was all over, we even became friends.

Concluding the Interview

Of course, you want the initial interview to end with the client retaining you and handing you a check or credit card. How do you get to that point? When you think you have all the information you need and have given the client whatever advice is appropriate, as them if they have any additional questions. Be sure that you leave them with the feeling that you have treated them with respect, listened attentively to their problem, and are genuinely interested in helping them solve it.

Sometimes a client will challenge you, as if they expect you to compete for their business. Occasionally at the end of the interview, they will ask you why they should hire you rather than someone else they've talked to. I always answered this question the same way. Unless the other lawyer was not a family lawyer, I wouldn't get involved in comparing myself to anyone else. I would explain to them that their legal problem is important, and the selection of a lawyer is probably the most important decision they will be called upon to make. Only they can decide who they are most comfortable with.

One good technique is to ask them what else they want to know about you. This was where I talked about my style, what I expected from them, and determined that we were on the same page. I would tell them that I am extremely organized, and would need them to commit to respond timely to my requests for information. I told them that I would give them lead time for non-emergency assistance I needed from them, but would expect them to get back to me in a reasonable time. I would explain this to them in terms of the benefit *to them*, not to me, that is, that I can't do the optimum job on their legal problem if I don't get the necessary information from them. I would emphasize that if they retained me, we would be working as a team, and maximum effectiveness would require good communication.

When (and how) to turn a client away

You don't *have* to take every potential client who consults with you. You don't even have to give them a reason, though it is nice if you can. When I had been practicing a couple of years, I once threw a prospective client out of my office because he wanted to skip out on his child support obligation. He consulted me to find out which states he could move to where a California child support order wouldn't be enforced. This was obviously in the Dark Ages, before federal intervention made this much more difficult. I refused to tell him. He asked if I knew which states they were (and of course I did). When I wouldn't tell him what they were, his response was that he was paying me and I had a duty to give him the information he wanted. I gave him back his check and escorted him to the door.

Other obviously undesirable clients are those who treat you unprofessionally, are rude to your staff, who make improper advances (and they do), or who make you feel uncomfortable for any reason. I once rejected a client who insisted on telling me in detail about the sexual problems which had led up to the divorce with his wife, despite the fact that I told him it was irrelevant to the case and he should be talking to a counselor instead. He clearly had his own agenda, and that was talking about sex with me.

Any client who pulls out a timer at the beginning of your consultation is a reject. He's assuming that you will cheat him by inflating your time records. If you let him get away with it, you're tacitly admitting that he's right to be suspicious.

Any client who asks you to do anything unethical is toast. So are the following:

- Any client who asks you to conceal evidence.
- Any client who conceals or destroys evidence himself.
- Any client who admits that he's been concealing property in preparation for the divorce and refuses to disclose it now.
- Any client who refuses to give you full and complete answers to questions which are relevant to his case.
- Any client who insists on bringing the kids to court.
- Any client who clearly can't afford you (unless you're willing to do it *pro bono*.)

Others aren't always so obvious. If they won't listen to you when you tell them something they don't want to hear, and imply that if you really *tried*, you could get it for them, you'll never satisfy them. Frankly, if they won't listen to you, that's a red flag. Communication never gets better than it is at the beginning of the case, and if it isn't good then, you're in big trouble.

A client who questions your hourly rate and tries to negotiate a lower one is not going to pay you. Presumably the fact that you are new is already reflected in your rate. There's no reason to reduce it further, and if you do, it sends the message that you don't really believe you are worth the rate you are quoting. I once had a potential client suggest that I should do it for free because his case was unique and I'd be learning *so much* from it. Not!

Avoid the client who has had six prior lawyers (or even two), and claims that each was worse than the last. You'll never please this one, and may even get sued for something your predecessor did. Chances are, he'll fire you the first time you tell him something he doesn't want to hear. Even worse, he might not fire you and you're stuck in the case.

If they are asking you to fight for something they can't get under the law (and many new client appointments will start out exactly that way), tell them so. If they persist after you've told them why they can't win what they want you to go after, it's ok to tell them that they should look elsewhere for representation. You will not be able to satisfy them if they are asking for things the law doesn't provide: "I can't give you what you want from this proceeding." You can never please this kind of client, and you probably won't get paid for trying.

If you tell a client why he can't win what he is asking you to pursue, and he tells you that he consulted Larry the Lawyer Down the Street, who told him otherwise, he's lying. If Larry had really told him that, he would have retained Larry and wouldn't be interviewing you.

If your communication with the client sucks you can say "In order to be successful in reaching your goals, we need to work together as a team; it isn't anybody's fault, but I don't feel we are communicating clearly enough to work effectively together."

If they want to litigate the value of the light bulbs left in the family home, or the meat in the freezer, and you've told them it isn't cost effective, you can say "You seem to want a level of litigation that I don't think is in your best interests, will result in legal fees out of proportion to the value to be obtained, and will cost you credibility with the judge on more substantive issues. If you're serious about taking this course, I think you need to find another lawyer."

If a case is clearly out of your league, or if your office and staffing aren't sufficient to meet the demands of a high profile case, there's no shame in telling a client, "I'm not set up to handle a case like this, but I can refer you to a couple of other lawyers who are." Now, there's a caveat here. Every case is new at this stage, and you've got to learn somehow. I hadn't been in practice more than six months before an extremely complex interstate child abduction custody case landed in my lap. I managed to learn as I went along. However, if someone with a chain of thirty-two fast food franchises walks into your office, you're probably not qualified to handle it at this stage. Give them the names some of the heavy hitters in your area. Better yet, call the heavy hitter yourself while the client is in the office and refer the case on the spot. The client will know you have his best interests at heart, and the heavy hitter will know that you know your limitations, and because you showed such good judgment, may well put you on his referral list for smaller cases he rejects.

Sometimes it's a case you love, but the timing is wrong. When I was in practice, I was a sucker for a really tough custody case. I also knew I could only handle one at a time, and needed a breather between them. There were times I got a call from a potential new client and I would say "I love your case, but I just finished a similar one, and I'm not ready emotionally to handle another one right now." And if they say "I'll wait for you" tell them not to. Their case is important and they might be jeopardizing their legal position by waiting, especially if you don't know when you'll be ready or when your workload will lighten up. They may wait anyway, but you won't be the one responsible if they suffer adverse consequences as a result of the delay.

Why refusing to accept a client who wanted to write me a big check that day was one of the smartest client development moves I ever made

Here's an interesting one: The client clearly doesn't want a divorce, but wants to send an ultimatum to the other side. As a result, they want you to file it *today*. This is a recipe for an unhappy client. The urgency is probably driven by a fear that she'll chicken out if she gives herself a chance to think about it. Maybe her friends are telling her "*I* wouldn't put up with that. How can *you?*" If you file the divorce she obviously doesn't want, she'll ultimately blame you.

Not giving in to this one turned out to be one of the best client development tools I ever used. About six months into practice, I was consulted by a woman who was clearly distraught, had just found out her husband was having an affair, and wanted me to file for divorce that day. I refused, telling her it was clear to me that she didn't really want a divorce; she wanted to send him a message. I told her that she could go down the street and find any number of lawyers who would file it for her, but I wouldn't, and suggested counseling and a cooling off period instead.

I practiced and lived in what was then a small town, and for years thereafter I would run into her in restaurants and stores. I never acknowledged her first, of course, because I didn't know if the person she was with knew that she had consulted me. Usually, she would find a way to sidle up to me and let me know that they were still working on the marriage. In the next ten years, she probably sent me fifteen clients, all of whom were good cases and nice people. She had told all of them the story and they were impressed by the fact that I wouldn't file a divorce I didn't think the client really wanted, even though she insisted and would have been happy to pay me to do it.

And remember, there will always be more clients if you do what is right.

How not to reject a client

Although it may not seem like it now when you are just starting out, you will have to learn how to reject a potential client. Don't just quote a high retainer, hoping they can't pay it. That's how I got the client who stalked me, sent me multiple death threats, and made my life a living hell for months. My gut didn't feel right when the guy consulted me. He didn't have much money but insisted he wanted me and only me to represent him. I thought that if I quoted a high retainer, he wouldn't be able to raise it. Instead, he borrowed the money, and I had a nut case on my hands and not much of a life for the next year.

Unless their case is unusually complex and exceeds the resources of your office and staff, don't tell them you're "too busy" to take their case. If you were too busy to take on new business, why didn't you tell them before you made the appointment for the interview and wasted their time? If you've already screened the case on the phone, you've had an opportunity to determine whether it can be integrated into your current case load, and the client knows it.

If you decide not to take a case, always be as honest as you can be, within the bounds of courtesy. This theme runs through all client relations. The question is not whether you will tell them the truth or not. It is simply how you do it. The only time you are not required to be courteous is when a prospective client has asked you to do something unethical. If that happens, don't sugar coat it. Unapologetically tell them they've insulted and offended you, and you are not willing to work with them. Someone who insults my integrity doesn't get much courtesy from me.

And if you reject the client, don't charge him for your time. It's not *his* fault you decided not to take the case.[10]

The good news about doing a thorough intake and screening these folks out is that you will have more time to deal with the good clients, the reasonable people, who simply need guidance getting through a tough time, and will be grateful for your help.

---

10 If he consults with you and then retains someone else, that's different and you're entitled to be paid for your time unless you've advertized "free initial consultation." Collect for the consultation at the end of the appointment, because you're not likely to get paid for your time if you wait and send a bill three weeks later for a one-shot consultation.

Five

KEEPING CLIENTS

OK, you've signed up the client. Now what? Part of the art of being a good and successful lawyer is keeping clients satisfied. You want to do a good job. You want to get paid, and you want your clients to send their friends to you. Many lawyers are lousy at client relations. Don't be one of them.

Never interrupt one client to deal with another. They are paying for and entitled to your attention. If you are doing trial preparation, it is extremely intense. If a client insists on interrupting you, instruct your staff to say "when preparing for trial, he gives a case his undivided attention. I'm sure you will want your case to have the same undivided attention when he's preparing for *your* trial."

Always take client phone calls if you are available, and return them promptly if you are not. The same is true for emails.

Research on litigant satisfaction with the courts illustrates a key client relations issue. The California Judicial Council did a survey of litigants in 2005. What they found was that if people feel heard, they are less concerned about whether they actually won or not. The sense of procedural due process, that is, that their rights were respected and they got a fair chance at court, was more important than outcome to the majority of those surveyed.

The bottom line is that if a client feels that his case is important to you, that you treat him and his legal problems with respect, he will be much more likely to accept the outcome, whether he "won" or not, and to send his friends to you.

Setting Boundaries

Your professional relationship with your client is just that: *professional.* That means that you have to know how to set and maintain boundaries. You may become friends with former clients. I've developed some important friendships that way. The operative term is "former" clients. Don't be friends while the case is going on. It may well get in the way of your objectivity, a quality which is essential to a successful professional relationship. Keep your relationship professional rather than personal and concentrate on the client's needs until the case is over.

Don't share personal info with your clients. You want to be courteous and make small talk with clients. However, the focus should be on them, and their problem, not on you. They may want to know if you have kids, especially if custody is an issue in their case. Beyond that, limit small talk to the times when you are ushering a client into your office, or out. This isn't sisterhood; it's business. They won't want to pay you for the time it takes to chit-chat (and they shouldn't), and it will come back to haunt you in fee arbitration: "He spent the whole time telling me about his trip to France (reciting the details you shared verbatim); why should I have to pay for that?" Of course, you *didn't* spend the whole time telling him about the trip, and probably didn't bill him for the time you did spend talking about it, but he'll forget all the legal advice you gave him (which he may have ignored), will remember every detail of the personal info you shared, and it will sound terrible at the arbitration.

If you do make small talk at the beginning of your consultation, keep it short, then look at your watch and say "Let's turn on the clock now and talk about your case."

If you make small talk at the end, look at your clock, say "Now we're off the clock" and have a brief conversation. Beware, though, that as soon as the client thinks the clock is off, he'll think of three more substantive things to ask you about. If you're going to bill him for it, tell him you have to turn the clock back on. If you don't intend to bill for it, keep it short.

Accessibility issues

Never give a client your home phone number or cell phone number unless you are willing to be available 24/7. Before giving out your cell phone number, think seriously about the level of intrusiveness you are willing to tolerate, and develop strategies for setting boundaries. For example, you may turn the cell phone off after hours, or use a different number for client calls. If you do, tell them the hours that you won't be available, so that they know whether to expect an immediate call back.

If you represent the parent of someone on your son's soccer team, you'll be "working" at every game and practice. Besides, your home phone number is on the parent's roster. You may decide that this is a good way to build a practice, and it may be. But you'll pay a price in lost privacy. If they insist on discussing their case at practice, tell them that your work is confidential and you can't discuss it in public where others might overhear. That way you are framing the issue in terms of explaining that what they are doing is harming *them*, and it is more courteous than the truth, which is that they are abusing the personal relationship and probably trying to get legal advice for free.

The same goes for the client you run into at Costco or the gas pump. That isn't the time or place to discuss their case. Use it to set up a time when you can speak privately.

If someone does have your home number and abuses it, set boundaries. Tell them "I'm sorry, but I can't take this type of call at home. I need to be at the office where I have your files in front of me and can refer to them." One way to nip this in the bud is to be sure you bill for the time you spent on the phone call at home when you get into the office. Be conservative in reporting the time, but report it. When it shows up on the bill, they may get the message. Better yet, make sure the bill identifies it as "telephone call at home."

Hand holding

Don't be a therapist. The client who just wants reassurance and therapy rather than advice or substantive legal work is a disaster waiting to happen. They may by in extreme crisis. They may want to connect daily, or even several times a day. That isn't your job, and if you do it, expect them to dispute the bill when the divorce is over and they've forgotten how needy they were at the time. Develop a way to tell them they're wasting your time and their money: "I'm a first rate attorney and a third rate therapist. You can get a first rate therapist for less than you're paying me, and I'm not qualified to deal with these issues in any event." Then refer them to several qualified therapists.

I guarantee that if you cross this line, there will be a fee dispute. They will object to your bill, saying, "It wasn't worth it." And they'll be right. I learned this one the hard way, when the partner I worked for had a particularly needy client. She was constantly dropping by, and he didn't want to deal with her, so of course, I was nominated to do the required hand holding. And since I was accountable for my hours, and had strict instructions to bill for everything, I did so. When the client disputed the bill, guess who was chosen to defend the fee arbitration? Of course, the partner was too busy. And although I was just following orders and doing what my boss and the client *both* insisted I should be doing at the time, the client successfully disputed the bill and I learned never to do it that way again.

This is just one of those areas where you must learn to set and maintain boundaries with your client. You are the professional. He isn't. And while you are cognizant of the emotional strain inherent in family law matters, and presumably took that into account in choosing this specialty, you still must maintain the boundaries and refuse to spill over into a therapist's role. Ditto for your staff.

How to keep communication flowing

Poor communication is the number one reason for sour attorney/client relationships. It's a snap to communicate good news to someone. It may be easier to give even bad news to someone you like. As professionals, we are often called upon to give very bad news. And sometimes we don't like the person we represent. That's when things get sticky.

Look the client in the eye. This is especially important if the news is bad. You have to tell them the truth, even if it's hard. Even if they really, really, really don't want to hear it. Even if they fire you for telling them the truth. Better that they fire you (or even blame you) than that they sue you for not telling them the truth or for putting a positive spin on the unspinnable. Human nature being what it is, they will always want to put the most positive interpretation on what you tell them. That means that if you tell them bad news in a wishy-washy way, they will latch on to the positive implications and disregard the negative. An important part of your job is to tell them what they should concede and where they should draw the line and stand firm. If they haven't gotten the message that they are going to lose something because you said it in an equivocal way, they are certain to blame you, not themselves. Of course, even if you tell them the truth and they refuse to believe you, they may still blame you. But at least you've done your professional best.

There's always a gentle way to tell the truth, though you may have to be creative to find it. And if the reason the news is bad is that your client was lying through his teeth, don't "explain" it by telling him the judge screwed up. That just makes him wonder why you didn't try to get the case to another judge. It's ok to say "The judge apparently didn't believe you." It isn't necessary to add that *you* didn't believe him either.

Don't spin it. If a client is likely to lose, tell him so. And when you give him the bad news about why he can't win and he asks the question "Whose side are you *on*, anyway?" tell him, "Yours. I'm not paid to lie to you. My job is to tell you the truth, even if we both wish it were different."

When waiting around the courthouse for a hearing, we frequently get to observe other attorneys in action. We may be sharing a bench with an attorney who is in the process of telling bad news to his client. I've said before that I've often added and deleted attorneys from my referral list based on how they handled this one task. I can't count the number of times I've heard an attorney telling a client that the judge isn't buying their position, whereupon the client asks "Does this mean we're going to lose?" Now, that's a perfectly straightforward question, and deserves a similarly straight answer. All too often, the attorney waffles at this point. Mind you, it usually isn't because the attorney is a jerk who wants to fleece this client for the fees he will charge to try the unwinnable case. Rather, he wants to convey good news and nobody taught him how to convey bad. The correct response is to look the client in the eye, and say "Yes, it looks that way," followed by suggestions for alternate strategies or compromising the losing issue in exchange for something else.

And don't forget that someone else is always listening and forming judgments about you when you are talking to *your* client in a crowded hallway at the courthouse.

All of these rules are ten times more important if you don't really like your client and don't think he *should* win. We don't get to interview both parties to a case and decide which one we would prefer to represent. We're stuck with the one who called us first. And the truth is we don't always get to represent the good guy. That's no excuse for poor communication. The unfortunate fact is that the harder it is to communicate with a client, the more important it is that you do it clearly, honestly and carefully.

Tools for success with the disorganized client

If you suspect that your client is disorganized, it is a good idea to give them an empty file folder, with instructions to put all of the correspondence and other paperwork they get from you in the file for easy reference. That means fewer clients will bring you documents in shopping bags, and file folders are cheap in relation to the frustration of trying to communicate with someone who throws your letters into the junk drawer or a pile of mail on the dining room table. On occasion, I insisted that the client buy one of those plastic document carriers with a handle and bring it to all appointments. That way I knew that they were gathering all important documents in a single place, and it was easy to get them to refer to it.

What do you mean there are weaknesses in my case?

I've talked about this before. Always look at your client's case with a critical eye. There are lots of reasons why this is important. The client is probably putting the best spin on the facts she's telling you. That's human nature. It is your job to ask the questions required to ferret out any other relevant facts she hasn't told you, especially if they are likely to lead to an unfavorable result. One simple way to do this is to ask, after hearing their story, "That's interesting. Now tell me what the other side is likely to say when I confront them with these facts." The result can be as benign as "I don't have a clue" and run the gamut to a sheepish admission that "he'll probably say that I shoved him first." This is information you need to have in advance.

Another useful question is "what is the worst thing the other side is going to say about you?" They often know exactly what it is. The client's credibility (and ultimate success) is likely to turn on whether you can prove the facts you allege in your paperwork.

Sometimes your client is flat lying to you. Never believe everything they say just because they are consulting you. Now, I'm not saying that you should assume every client lies. However, if the story they tell you doesn't seem to hang together, there's probably a reason. If there are unanswered questions, ask them. Ask for verification of questionable information. It's easy to do this without seeming to call your client a liar. One of your jobs is to develop evidence, so it is natural to ask what data or witnesses he has to support his position when you present it to the judge, as in, "That is interesting. What documents do you have/can you get that I can use in evidence to corroborate your testimony? What witnesses will support your version of what occurred?" You're not calling him a liar when you do this;

you're preparing his case. Although you may still get burned occasionally, you will ultimately develop a sixth sense for when something doesn't pass the sniff test.

There's another reason for doing this: your opponent will be looking for all the weaknesses in your case. Isn't it better to dig them out yourself than to be blindsided in court because you took your client's version of the facts on faith?

There's a subtext to this. Our job as advocates is to present our client's case in the best light. That doesn't mean suspending all judgment ourselves.

Nine things NEVER to say to a client

Most lawyers are relatively bright people, but some of them sure say stupid things to clients. I have known at least one attorney to say each of the following to his/her client:

1. "I've never handled this issue before. This is great! I'll learn right along with you."

Of course, you're new, and there's a first time for everything. But this statement was made by an attorney with over ten years' experience. I can't imagine how she thought this would play with her potential client. The client understandably became concerned that she'd picked the wrong professional and went looking for someone who *had* handled it before (me) and wouldn't be learning on her dime.

2. "I don't do math. That's why I have a forensic accountant" or even worse "If I could do math I would have gone to medical school instead of law school."

Honest, I heard an attorney say this in front of a client whose entire case turned on the tracing of complicated financial transactions. The attorney made it clear that she was deferring this function entirely to the forensic accountant and didn't understand the case herself. Now, how does the client process that information? If the attorney is lucky and the client is an idiot, there may be no intellectual processing going on at all. But if she isn't, the client has just been put on notice that the person whom she is trusting to protect her financial interests has no knowledge or expertise, and little interest, and is delegating all of those matters to a non-lawyer. This is a malpractice suit waiting to happen, especially if the client is greedy and doesn't think she came out of the divorce with as much as she was "entitled" to.

3. "Sorry to keep you waiting. I was stuck on the phone with a client who is a real pain in the rear."

Never refer to one client disparagingly of another. Period. They will wonder what you say about them behind their back.

4. "I can usually get what I want from Judge Granitehead."

It may be true. You're an idiot if you say so. Your client is sure to tell his spouse that you have the judge in your pocket. And what if this is the time Judge Granitehead decides that *you're* the doofus?

Corollary: "Judge Granitehead can't stand Joe Nitpicker" (your opposing counsel). Or "Joe Nitpicker isn't very bright." Your client will call his wife in minutes to gloat that she's going to lose at court.

Telling your *client* that your opponent is an idiot is tantamount to telling your opponent to his face. Expect to get a call from Joe tomorrow demanding an apology. Then expect Joe to put on the case of a lifetime to prove that you're wrong.

5. "The forensic accountant on the other side doesn't know a Schedule C from Vitamin C."

That also may be true. What possible benefit is there in telling your client that he won because the other expert (or attorney, for that matter) is an idiot, rather than because you're so good? And if you've just picked your opponent's pocket because he's a bonehead, how smart is it to tell your own client, who will probably gleefully repeat what you said verbatim to his spouse the next time they exchange the kids?

6. "Your wife is a real idiot."

Your client may share your opinion. He may have just expressed it himself. However, the idiot you're referring to is the someone he chose to have children with. What does that say about his judgment? Chances are, even if he agrees with you, he'll feel insulted.

7. "Your wife/husband is really good looking."

Your client will immediately assume you have the hots for the opposing party and will throw the case for them. Be very, very careful of what you say to your client about the opposing party, either positive or negative.

8. "What on earth prompted you to marry him/her?"

This goes back to #6. No one likes to have their nose rubbed into their own poor judgment. In fact, he'd prefer to think it wasn't poor judgment at all, but rather that Dr. Jekyll turned into Ms. Hyde after he married her.

9. "I guarantee we can't lose on this."

Unless the issue is the Anti-Heart Balm statute of 1912 or the Thirteenth Amendment, be very careful about guaranteeing a win. You aren't Joe Namath and the result isn't entirely under your control. There's lots of gray area out there, and judges occasionally make bad decisions. Instead, say "the law is pretty clear on this point" or "sometimes judges do something unaccountable, but I've never seen that argument (that the other side is making) prevail. I think we have a very good chance of winning this at court."

Things never to say about a client to someone else (especially the judge)

1. "My client is an idiot."

I'm sorry. Your client may be the doofus of the Western world. Never disparage your client to opposing counsel or the court. I know more than one attorney who routinely does this. They must assume it is being collegial to swap client stories with colleagues or in chambers. It isn't. It's being stupid and unprofessional. It also raises the bar on malpractice. If your client is really that dumb, maybe he can't give informed consent to the deal you've just worked out. Where does that leave *you?* And if the comment is made to opposing counsel, assume she will repeat it to her client and it will get back to *your* client.

2. "My client is unsophisticated."

This is a variation on the last one. Your client may be as dumb as the proverbial post, but don't label her in court papers. You can say that your client didn't handle the money in the marriage, that she was primarily responsible for the children, that he relied on others to manage his money, but call him clueless at your peril. It is insulting, and will be quoted back to him by the opposing party, and probably to the children. Instead, stick to the facts without ascribing labels.

If your client truly is impaired, and it is important to state that in court papers because it impacts legal rights and responsibilities, you have another issue. If the impairment impacts ability to give consent, you may need a conservator or guardian *ad litem* in order to proceed. And of course, beware of the client who claims impairment as long as it benefits him by giving him an excuse from being required to go to work, but insists on orchestrating the case in every aspect. Putting a statement in court papers that your client is clueless simply raises the bar for *your* performance on his case. You're asking him to blame you for any adverse result (read: any result he doesn't understand, which will be *most* results). Instead, state the facts and lose the pejorative conclusions.

3. "My client can't get over the break up."

Whether said to the judge or opposing counsel, this sends the message that your client's positions are driven by emotional factors rather than appropriate legal grounds, and seriously undercuts the credibility of your position. Blaming the emotional condition of your client for the conduct of the case is perilous in the extreme. It also suggests that you are merely a cipher, carrying out your client's instructions, rather than the professional you are.

How to refuse to do something a client wants you to do

These issues fall into a number of categories. Sometimes it's as benign as whether or not to grant the other side a professional courtesy which won't negatively impact your client's interests. Sometimes it's something unethical. Both of these are no-brainers. But there's a lot of gray area in between.

Sometimes a client wants to dictate the strategy or procedures. I never allowed that. I'm the one who knows the courts, the procedures, and the like. I'm the one with professional training, and responsibility for the result. I wouldn't be doing my job if I delegated those things to a non-professional. The client and I set the goals, but I set the strategy on how to get there, and I am sole arbiter of procedure. If he and I are definitely not on the same page, maybe he needs another attorney.

Sometimes the client sees another lawyer in court and decides he wants you to be more flamboyant, or combative, or whatever he admires in the other attorney's style. When that happened to me, I would tell him, "I'm a first rate Sue Talia and a third rate _____ (fill in the name of anybody other than Sue Talia). I won't be as effective if I try to adopt someone else's style. If that is what you want, maybe you need to hire him instead of me." And if he takes you up on it, thank your lucky stars. You weren't going to satisfy him, because he didn't want *you*.

Sometimes what the client wants you to do is just plain stupid. I had a case once where my client was insisting that I subpoena records which would prove that her husband had lied over a $600 item. I estimated that the subpoena would cost $800, and refused. We went round and round about this, with me pointing out that we had ample other evidence that hubby was a liar, and there was no reason to spend more than the issue was worth just to add cumulative evidence. I ultimately told her that if she wanted that subpoena sent out, she'd have to get another lawyer. She gave in, we did it my way, and we cleaned up on the case at trial. This is the kind of thing that, if you cave on, will always come back to haunt you in fee arbitration. One of your jobs is to do the cost/benefit analysis that your client is incapable of doing because he's just too emotionally invested in the conflict to make good judgments.

What if you're getting sucked into the client's agenda and losing your objectivity?

This is a tough one. Try to step back and look at the case from the other side. There are always two sides to every story, especially when there are only two "witnesses," and nothing is so subjective and susceptible to differing interpretations than the quicksand of intimate relationships. Also, even the biggest jerk in the world may have *some* redeeming qualities.

Don't let your client's crusade become *your* crusade. One of the major temptations facing family lawyers is to adopt a "White Knight" role, where you decide that you alone are responsible for rescuing your poor client from the brute who has been abusing her, literally or figuratively. It's ok to want to help, to want to fix it to the extent that you can, and to be the one to step up for the client's rights when she can't. That is all part of being an effective advocate. However, when you set out to "save" a client from the consequences of his or her past choices, you step over the line. It is almost impossible to retain any objectivity when this is the focus you bring to the case. There are several dangers which result. First, your desire to avenge the wrong may blind you to a reasonable settlement offer. It then may become your agenda, not the client's. She (and it is often "she" but not always) may really need to quickly get the best deal she can, and then walk away from the conflict. If you've strapped your armor on and are entering the jousting fields, you may not recognize this. Instead of resolving the issue, the likely result is that the other party engages with you instead of your client, and the conflict escalates to the further detriment of your client.

Another pitfall of becoming over involved emotionally in the client's problem is that it may prevent you from providing a very important service:

teaching the client how to resolve his or her own problems in the future. I've spent countless hours teaching decision-making skills to clients who were powerless in the marriage. I would tell them that I would spend as much time as they needed to show them how to evaluate their options, and review the pros and cons of a particular resolution, but I couldn't make the decision whether to sell the house, fight for or give up custody, or whatever, because *they* would be living with the consequences of that decision for years and I would be long gone. I told them that part of the service I performed was to teach them the skills to evaluate a settlement offer or make a financial decision, so that they could do it with confidence after the case was done and I was out of the picture. If you're on a crusade, you're too busy pursuing the conflict to teach your client how to avoid or resolve it in the future.

One of the least effective lawyers I know takes great pride in becoming emotionally invested in her client's cases. That's how she self-defines her role as an advocate. As a result, she has no insight into the weaknesses of her own case and is unable to advise the client when it is in his best interest to concede a weak point. That means that every aspect of the case has to be litigated to the nth degree and settlement is virtually impossible. If you really can't be objective, you may need to get out of the case.

How much of my strategy should I share with my client?

Sometimes clients just can't be trusted to know your strategy. It's amazing how many of them will run to their spouse and spill the whole thing. Even if they don't tell their spouse directly, they may post on Facebook or other social media, or run it by their friends. Divorcing couples often can't resist gloating over each other. It's stupid, but they do it. If you've just come up with a killer strategy, be careful how much of the detail you share with your client. And if you do, be sure to admonish them not to drop a hint of it to their best friend or their spouse. Word gets back.

It seems obvious, but never lie

Never lie *to* a client
Never lie *for* a client
Never lie to a judge
Never lie to an expert
Never lie to opposing counsel

Discussing other cases with your client

Never discuss other cases with your client except in the most sanitized way, and only for purposes of illustrating how the judge or opposing counsel acted in situation similar to theirs. They're not *that* stupid; they know that if you discuss someone else's case with them, there's a good chance you'll discuss *their* case with others as well. And it is amazing how small the world is. They may be best friends with your other client, or worse, the client's ex-wife.

This comes up all the time when a satisfied client refers a friend to you. The friend will usually tell you who referred them, and may directly or indirectly ask about their friend's case. Be very firm that you can't discuss their friend's case with them. Easily as often, the referring client will tell you "I gave your name to Joe Blow. Did he call you?" There is only one correct answer to that. "I appreciate the confidence you expressed in recommending me to your friend, but I can't discuss who might have consulted me. You'll have to ask Joe."

Give clients bad news verbally and personally

I may seem to be beating this one to death, but I know many readers of this book will not read it straight through, but skip from section to section. This one is just so important that I can't take a chance that it will be missed. Don't have your legal assistant call to tell your client that the judge's order just came in the mail and he lost. Don't just put a copy of the bad court decision in the mail with a letter telling him to call you to talk about it. Especially don't do this before a weekend or holiday, when he'll have to stew about it for a couple of days before he can talk to you and find out what it means for the rest of his case.

Instead, pick up the phone and call him and be prepared to tell him what (if anything) you believe can be done about it. And if nothing can be done about it, *say so*. Don't waffle. We all would love to be able to be the bearers of only good news. It ain't so, folks. But if you do it right, they won't blame the messenger. If you do it wrong, they will, even if the ruling makes it clear that the reason they lost is that the judge figured out they were lying their fool heads off.

If you and your client are in conflict and you have to tell him something unpleasant, such as setting boundaries for the case or his conduct, breakdowns in communication or the like, tell him verbally. If you think it is important to put into writing, then confirm with a letter *after* the personal conversation. Don't just lay it out in the letter so that the first time he sees it is on paper.

"Strong letter to follow"

Remember that letters, texts and emails always sound more harsh than verbal communications and emoticons are poor substitutes for nuanced verbal inflections. You may be furious with your client. Hold that "strong letter to follow" until you've had a chance to cool off. Ditto inflammatory letters to opposing counsel. 24 hours is a good cooling off period.

Computers are wonderful things, except in one regard. They make it far too easy to use bold face fonts and italics for emphasis. People hate getting letters which seem to scream at them. Lose the bold fonts, italics, and exclamation points in letters. They're offensive. If you've said it right, it won't need emphasis.

Swapping jokes in chambers

There will often be times when you and your opposing counsel are called into chambers to talk to the judge while the clients wait in the courtroom.

Never forget that they can sometimes hear what is said. Be very, very careful about laughter coming out of chambers. We all want the judges and opposing counsel to like us; it makes our job infinitely easier. But never forget that the clients are sitting tensely in the court room while their attorneys are meeting with the judge in chambers and discussing issues which are critically important to them out of their earshot. If they hear laughter coming from chambers, they are going to assume you're giving away the store or conspiring with the enemy. And what if the news you have to deliver to the client after that conference is bad? Your client will be sure you didn't strongly argue her position. Don't yuk it up with opposing counsel or the judge when your client is in earshot.

What to do when you see clients in public

Sooner or later, you'll run into a client at the grocery store or gas station. Be friendly and volunteer nothing. You don't know who is on the other side of the aisle or at the next gas pump. If they want to talk about their case, keep it brief, then suggest that they need to talk at a time when there is more privacy. Encourage them to call you to discuss it or to make an appointment.

Be particularly careful about seeing someone in public who looks familiar but whom you just can't place. You may be a friendly sort of person, but if you march up to her and say, "You look familiar. How do I know you?" you might find out that her kid was in school with yours some years ago. You might also find that she consulted you about a divorce last May and her spouse (standing within earshot) doesn't know. When in doubt, give them a friendly look which volunteers nothing and let them make the first move. If they ask why you didn't acknowledge them first, explain the foregoing. They will be grateful for your protection of their privacy.

Prepare anything which requires the client's signature well in advance

We're used to the court process and the deadlines for filing papers. Our clients aren't. They *hate* it when you've known for weeks that a document was due to be filed on the 12th at 4:00 p.m. and don't tell them until that morning, when they have to make an important presentation at work. It's simple courtesy to let them know that you will need them to sign something for filing with the court, and to give it to them with reasonable time to review and correct it.

It's even worse if you then say, "Where have you been? My staff has been trying all morning to find you" when they had no idea that papers were due at court today.

There's another reason: you may find out that the detailed declaration you've prepared at the last minute is inaccurate, and there's no time to correct it before the filing deadline.

Sometimes, through no one's fault, the story the client told you gets garbled in translation. You may remember details differently than they told you. You may put a spin on the facts in the retelling which distorts the result. This can happen to the best of us. We know which facts are most important to proving our case, and the temptation to pump them up a bit can be irresistible. It's one thing to accentuate the positive; it's another to put the wrong spin on it. If your client signs the declaration because there's no time to correct it, all you're doing is setting him up to be crucified on cross examination. He'll justifiably resent you if you made him sign a hurried declaration he can't defend on the stand and he loses credibility as a witness (or maybe even the whole case) when he can't back up the words that *you* put in his mouth.

Even if the error is corrected before the paperwork is filed, your client will be legitimately furious with you and conclude (correctly) that their legal document isn't very important to you, or you wouldn't have left it until the last minute. Always leave yourself time to fix it or fine tune it.

What to do with the client who tries to bully you

Sooner or later, someone will try. Many will try it on a new lawyer as a matter of course. Sometimes this is done to test you on the theory that if *they* can bully you, so can their spouse or the opposing attorney. Don't ever let them get away with it, or they'll own you. Call them on it and tell them that if it happens again, they'll be looking for another attorney. Tell them that you will treat them professionally and expect them to do the same with you. Or else.

What if the client bullies your staff instead? Don't let them get away with this, either. If a client is rude to a staff person, confront them with it and demand an apology. Make them deliver the apology to the staff person involved, not just to you. Unless they are complete jerks, they are usually very sorry and realize that they were taking out their frustrations on the wrong person. This usually nips the problem in the bud. If it doesn't, get rid of the client. Why should you or your staff accept abuse? If you do, the client won't respect you and you won't be able to keep good staff.

There's another reason to take a hard line here. The client who treats you unprofessionally doesn't respect you, and will probably resist paying you for your services, so you can expect to be eating your bill.

If you keep these simple rules in mind, you will vastly increase the chances that your clients will give glowing reports on your work. This will be conveyed to their family, friends, and the person who referred them. The result will be a much steeper curve from being a newbie just starting out to having the kind of practice you want to have. Remember, the goal of this is to have so many satisfied clients that you can be selective about the referrals you take. Then *you* will be on the lookout for the bright up and coming newbie to whom you can refer the overflow.

Six

Firing Clients

How to recognize the problem client and what to do about it

Many of these will be weeded out in the interview process. But what if you've already taken the case, or worse, your boss has taken the case and assigned it to you to work on? We all know what rolls downhill. All too many attorneys with new associates take marginal cases, knowing *they* won't have to deal with the problem client personally, and then delegate the case to the new associate to handle (usually accompanied by pressure to bill, bill, bill!). Unless the only reason to take the case is to protect a stellar referral source, this is a *terrible* business practice. Usually, the client resents being shunted off on the newbie when it was the partner he thought he was hiring. That means he already resents you. He is likely to second guess everything you tell him. He may complain to your boss. The short answer is that you're stuck.

Sometimes your boss didn't do it to you; you did it to yourself. We've all been there, and so will you: The client presented so well at the initial consultation, but turned into a two-headed monster. If you found out after the first hearing there may still be time to get out.

If you don't find out until it is too late, i.e., you can't get out without abandoning a client, there are still some things you can do to minimize the negative repercussions. Make sure your file is impeccably papered (this goes for the case your boss assigned you as well; at least your file will attest to the quality of your work even if the client isn't satisfied). Insist on payment as you go if at all possible. Sometimes that alone will weed out the problem client. Treat the case as the learning experience it has become and recognize that at this point you may be working for the experience, not the money. And ask the little voice that lives inside your head to warn you if you find yourself interviewing a potential client in the future who reminds you of this bozo.

Sometimes you can pay a problem client to go away. Well, sort of. If it is early enough in the case, it may be worth it to you to refund the retainer in exchange for their signing a substitution of attorneys.

Sometimes you can even do it in the middle of a case. I once had a hate/hate relationship with a client. We frankly acknowledged that we hated each other. She second guessed everything I did, and didn't really believe a woman could be as effective an attorney as a man. This was a problem, because my opposing counsel was of the male persuasion. No matter what we won, she assumed she would have won more if she had been represented by a man. Everything I did was minimized in her mind. If we won something, it was because we were *right* and the judge merely recognized the obvious, not because of anything *I* did. If we lost, it was because I hadn't done enough to convince the judge of the merits of her position, and not because I'd been telling my client for months that she was wrong and we weren't going to win that point.

There was literally no way to please her, and I told her it was clear that she needed a different attorney in whom she had more confidence, preferably a male since she didn't trust women. At the time, she owed me about $5,000, which coincidentally was about as much as it would have taken to retain another attorney. She told me she didn't have the money to hire someone else, though she agreed with me that our relationship had completely broken down. So I agreed to write off my bill if she would go away. Frankly, the relationship was so toxic that it was cheap at the price. She fired me and retained a grey-haired male attorney (whom she later made as miserable as she had made me). I don't recommend this as standard practice, and of course I should have known not to let her get into me for that much money. Nevertheless, it was a lesson well learned, and I never took her clone in the future.

Sometimes you can work a miracle for a client, and they think you sold them down the river. If you've gotten a good deal for your client, but she still doesn't think so, write her a letter explaining all the reasons why the settlement you negotiated was in her best interests.[11] I learned this from a wonderful judge who took me aside after we had negotiated s settlement of a particularly difficult case. Even though it was well after dinner time by the time we left the courthouse, he told me go straight to my office to dictate a letter to my client that very evening before going home. He cautioned me to be sure that the letter set out all the reasons why the settlement which we had reached was in her best interests, and describe in detail how much she had to lose by taking her case to trial. That letter saved my bacon, even though I didn't get home until very late that night. The judge recognized that my client was going to turn on me, but at the time I didn't have enough experience to see it for myself.

When that same client later decided that I *hadn't* done my job appropriately and consulted a series of lawyers over the next few months with the intention of suing me, all I had to do when they called me was send them a copy of that letter. I'm sure I couldn't have reconstructed that level of detail if I had waited until the next day to dictate it (when I was trying to return all the phone calls which had accumulated the day before, while I was stuck in court with Madame Trouble), much less a week later, or worse, when I got the first call questioning the result.

As time went on, and her "recollection" became more and more skewed, the fact that she had gotten a letter from me immediately after the fact, citing chapter and verse of what had actually happened (and which differed

---

11   And by the way, I wouldn't bill the client for the time I spent dictating this letter.

significantly from the version of events she was telling these attorneys) carried far more weight than her seller's remorse and second guessing. And it was particularly important in that case that it was a contemporaneous letter which was *sent to the client* rather than simply a self-serving memo to file which could have been created after the fact. As a result of that letter, no one would take the case against me, they all told her she didn't stand a chance of prevailing if she sued me, and most told her that she had gotten a good deal.

When and how to fire a client

It goes without saying that you can't abandon a client. If it's the eve of trial, you're stuck. The good news is that if you do a good job in court for the nutty client, the trial record itself will protect you.

If there's time, send the client a substitution of attorney, with a letter indicating that you intend to file a motion to withdraw if they don't sign and return it. I've fired clients for lots of things:

- For lying to me.
- For lying to the court.
- For lying in deposition.
- For refusing to respond to valid discovery requests.
- For concealing, destroying or fabricating evidence.
- For concealing property.
- For refusing to follow my advice when I felt the refusal was irreparably harming their position.
- For refusing to obey court orders when they had the ability to do so.
- For not paying me. [12]

When you fire a client, it is important to tell them why you are firing them, and frame it in the form of how their conduct is harming *them* and preventing you from doing your job *for them*.

"I can't effectively represent you if you don't tell me the truth."

---

12 Though in retrospect, I didn't use this one as much as I wish I had.

"You are required by law to provide these documents. If you refuse to do so, I cannot protect you from the sanctions which the court will impose on you."

"The actions which you are insisting on taking are directly contrary to my advice. I believe you are irreparably harming your legal position such that I cannot effectively represent you in the future."

"I am an officer of the court, and I won't be an accessory to perjury."

Usually, they signed the substitution, and that was the end of it. Of course, I ended up writing off whatever fees were unpaid, which is another reason not to let clients get too far ahead of you. But more about that in Chapter 11 on Billing.

And if you have to file a motion to withdraw, be very, very careful what you put into your declaration. You can't breach a confidence, so you can't say your client is a lying slimeball who intends to perjure himself at trial. Besides, the judge who is going to hear the motion to withdraw may well be the same judge who will hear the trial. It wouldn't do for you to prejudice the judge by telling her what a mendacious scumbag your client is. The universal catch-all "breakdown in communication" or "breakdown in the attorney/client relationship" is about as far as you can go in a public record.

Also, you have to be sure your withdrawal doesn't prejudice your client. There has to be plenty of time before trial. You have to turn over your file to new counsel and be sure they are advised of all deadlines. And don't get cheap about the photocopy expense: keep a complete copy of the file for yourself.

What if you really detest your client?

A good rule of thumb is that you should never represent someone you actively dislike. You will find excuses not to deal with him, or to deal only indirectly to the extent you can. This is almost a guarantee that things will slip through the cracks and is a recipe for malpractice.

Now, this is business, and I'm not suggesting that you only represent people you'd invite to dinner. There will be lots of people you don't particularly like or connect with whom you can represent competently and effectively. But if you actively detest them, you're in trouble. Note that these cases usually arise out of situations where you fail to set effective boundaries with your client.

Here's how not to do it. Suppose you hate your client and your client hates you. It is too late to get out of the case without abandoning the client. Neither of you wants to deal directly with the other. You arrange to always be "unavailable" when the client calls, and return the call to the home phone only when you know the client is at work. The client then gets the message after work and leaves a nasty after hours message on your voicemail or dashes off an incendiary email. Since you don't like dealing with each other, most communication is by letter or email. Here's what happens: your client gets home from work, finds the letter, and then calls and leaves a screaming message on your voicemail, often coupled with a nasty letter on the fax or an email in your inbox. This, of course, will ruin your day the moment you walk into the office, or worse, ruin your evening if you check email on your phone. The escalation of this passive/aggressive minuet is that you respond either with a phone message (at the number where the client won't answer) or another letter, and the beat goes on. And, of course, the bill never gets paid.

A more effective way to handle this, and an ultimately less painful one, would be to set a time when the two of you can meet face to face, and hash it out in person, including the possibility that the client should sign a substitution of attorney and find someone else with whom they are more compatible. That meeting won't be loads of fun, but it addresses the problem at the root and carries at least a chance of a satisfactory resolution.

There's another reason to avoid representing people you detest: If you don't like them, they probably know it. Such a strong feeling is rarely a one way street. If you detest her, she probably detests *you*, too. (Remember the client I paid to go away?) She is only putting up with you as long as she needs to because it is too late in the case to change lawyers or she doesn't want to have to raise another retainer. She'll keep you in the case as long as she needs you, and then she will refuse to pay you.

Working with these clients will do a number on your quality of life. And even if you are successful in concealing your dislike and they pay you for your work, they'll send you their friends, who are just like them. Who needs it? You'll hate their friends, too.

The most dangerous client there is

The poster child for the dangerous client is someone who is

Entitled
Angry
Stupid
Vengeful

This is a combination made in hell. You will never be able to give them what they want, and they will blame you.

How to spot the Client from Hell

We've all been there: you take a perfectly good case with a presentable client from a good referral source. The story sounds plausible, and all goes well until you make that first call to opposing counsel. As you hear them recite their client's version of the facts, the hair starts to stand up on the back of your neck as you realize you have a serious problem client. You should assess your options for getting out of the case. If it is too late to get out, all you can do is pray that they pay their bills and you'll recognize their clone the next time.

We all know the usual rules: don't be attorney #4, don't be pressured by a stated "emergency" which prevents a thorough intake interview, don't let a family member (usually a parent of your client, but not always) dictate the strategy, etc. But what about the more subtle indicators? Here are a few to watch out for. The Client from Hell usually has several of the following characteristics:

- Does not want a level playing field

They tend to be dishonest and devious. They want to limit and parse the information they dole out to you and to the other side. They are secretive and suspicious of why you need so much information about "their business," and resist providing the evidence you've requested to support their assertions. They try to keep you on a "need to know" basis, and in their minds, you don't need to know very much.

- Is greedy

They don't want you to tell them what they are entitled to. They want to know what angles you can play to get them more than that, and what kind of "evidence" would help you do that (presumably so they can go out and try to manufacture it).

- Is domineering

They were probably domineering in the marriage, and will likely carry that charming personality trait into their dealings with you. They will want to dictate all aspects of the process, and don't appreciate your "interference." They come with a ready-made strategy of how things are and how they are going to be, and aren't interested in whether you share their opinion. This category includes not only the domineering client, but the parent or new spouse who insists on controlling the action.

- Is entitled

They fell into a sweet deal, either by indulgent parents (who may still be taking care of them), inheritance, marriage, or a fortuitous investment, and they expect you to ensure that the sweet deal continues for life, regardless of the legalities, and especially regardless of whether their spouse has a claim to part of the sweet deal. And remember, there is no one more entitled than someone who didn't work for what it is they are trying to hold on to.

- Is impatient

They expect everything to be done yesterday and for the case to be over in a matter of weeks, and will not understand why you cannot make it so.

- Is suspicious

They will question the motives and integrity of the experts, the judge, the witnesses, and ultimately, *you*, and if they don't get what they want (however many times you told them it was unrealistic) will see a conspiracy to defraud them at every turn.

- Has an ax to grind

They will come in with reams of vitriol they've pulled off the web which "demonstrates" that the legal system is biased against their particular demographic (and since there is so much lunacy on the web, they're sure to find something to support their position). The first time they don't get what they want, they will threaten to "go public" with the perceived bias. These are the ones who picket outside the courthouse, complain about you to the State Bar, post hateful reviews on Yelp and other websites, and ultimately sue you.

- Is guilty over the breakup

You'd think these would be good clients, willing to give more than they should to assuage their guilt. It is a recipe for disaster. They give too much at the beginning. They expect a gold star from the other side for their generosity, which of course never comes. Remember, they're guilty, so the other side naturally feels wronged, and feeling entitled is never far behind feeling wronged. The recipient of the overly generous initial agreements expects the benefits to continue. A colleague of mine is fond of saying that "guilt has a very short half life." When the half life of guilt expires, the guilty client will want to recoup what they already gave away (against your advice), and will go to the mattresses over stupid issues they can't win. The other side of the double whammy is that the recipient of the guilt-induced largesse has started to feel entitled to it (see #4) and will resent mightily any attempt to substitute a more reasonable and realistic division of the goodies, support, or whatever the issue is. You are highly unlikely to get paid by these clients, and will spend far too much of your time fighting over minutiae.

- Is utterly innocent

They can't think of a single thing *they* might have done which contributed to the failure of the relationship. Their spouse is a "pathological liar," or a "Jekyll and Hyde" such that there was NO WAY they, or anyone else for that matter, could have seen through the facade until the ultimate blow-up. They demonize the other party (and this goes beyond normal anger and hurt). If you suggest they go to counseling to deal with the reasons for the breakup, or just their own strong feelings, they accuse you of not being on their side.

- Is bitterly resentful

Anger, disappointment and hurt feelings are normal. Bitter, corrosive and unrelenting resentment is not. Run the other way. It won't be long before they are resenting *you*. In the words of one judge of my acquaintance, they will attempt to reexamine every transaction of the marriage "through a glass darkened by the deep disappointment of marital failure."

- Is crafty

These people have some "dirt" on the other side and start out with "I don't want to use this unless I *have* to, but….." What follows is usually a story of tax fraud, skimmed earnings, kickbacks, or the like. Actually, the larceny was probably just fine with them when *they* were the beneficiaries. What they can't stand is that the new lover is getting the benefits now.

- Avoids dealing with the divorce

Sometimes they are up front about this and specifically ask you to drag it out as long as possible, in hopes the other side will change their mind. This is bad enough, because as it drags on, they will have a million reasons why they can't pay you until it is over. Guess whose legal fees start to accumulate into a monumental account receivable? It's even worse if they aren't up front about it. They will simply avoid the process, avoid *you,* not respond to your letters and phone calls, and leave you to explain it to the judge.

- Alienates the kids

Sometimes they are savvy enough to be underground about this, but it is amazing how many people will volunteer to their attorney how much they hate the other parent, and proudly announce that "the kids hate him, too." Another red flag: If your client refers to the other parent as "Hitler," "Osama," or "the Wicked Witch of the West," that's your cue to exit stage left.

- Didn't pay their prior attorney(s)

Of course, some clients will come to you because they were badly represented, or overcharged, and may have a legitimate fee dispute with prior counsel. This isn't universal, however. If they have unpaid prior attorneys, look very, very carefully at them before agreeing to take the case. Consider that they may have been fired by prior counsel for unreasonableness and failure to pay. That's not a conga line you want to join.

Seven

You and Your Staff

S taff issues fall into two categories: What happens when you hire staff yourself and are responsible for them, and what happens when somebody else hires and supervises them. We will start with the first, and then talk about the special problems which arise when you have little or no control over your own staff.

How much staff do I really need?

Don't hire more staff than you can keep consistently busy. You don't need to have someone sitting by the front door in your office to look important. Hire only as much staff as you absolutely need. Remember, you'll be doing a lot of your own work on the computer. It is always more efficient to hire a temporary person to do a specific project which exceeds your staff capacity than to hire too many people and have them underutilized. Voicemail works fine as a receptionist, as long as you return your calls promptly.

How much do I pay them?

After you've decided how much staff you *absolutely* need, hire the best quality person you can find and pay them well. It's always better to have a quality part timer than a full time slug. I once went from a full time legal assistant to one who worked only four hours a day. I nearly had a heart attack when the part timer quoted her minimum hourly rate. Turns out, she was so efficient that I saved money and had a superb quality work product.

If they're not cutting it, let them go as soon as you figure it out, and find someone else. Do it kindly, but do it. If you don't, you'll find yourself saddled with bad employees for years because they've been there too long to fire without incurring a wrongful termination lawsuit. Stands to reason: If inferior work was fine for the first three years, why is it suddenly unacceptable now?[13]

The Gospel According to Aretha

Always treat your staff with respect. Be friendly, considerate and professional, and expect the same from them. It's business. As with clients, it is important to set boundaries. If your office turns into sisterhood, you're bound to have personnel problems.

Treat them as part of the team. That's exactly what they are. If you treat them like minions, they'll resent it and you'll get inferior service. Pretty soon, no one good will work for you and it will show in the quality of your office output.

Insist your clients and opposing counsel also treat your staff courteously.

When I first began, I worked for a firm which had a ridiculously hierarchical policy that all attorneys were to be addressed formally, as "Mr." or "Mrs." (It was so old fashioned that "Ms." was out of the question!) The staff members, of course, were referred to by first names. It was ludicrous that overnight I went from law clerk "Sue" to attorney "Mrs." It was even worse because the firm had never had a woman lawyer before, and everyone resented it. Fortunately, I had worked with these people, and knew that they knew a

---

13 And it doesn't help in the wrongful termination lawsuit if your defense is that for the first three years you were still learning yourself, so you didn't know good work from bad.

lot of things that I didn't. I let it be known what I thought of the policy by referring to my own legal assistant as "Mrs. Davis." Ultimately, the policy was changed, but in the interim I made it clear that respect was a two way street.

Training isn't optional

Take the time to train staff well. Be clear about the quality of work you expect. Give them reasonable lead time, and call their attention to mistakes immediately. Don't do it rudely, but don't let it slide, either. Be matter of fact. Tell them why the way they did it is wrong, and how it should be done in the future. Don't just fix it yourself, or they will never learn.

Always make sure *you* know how to do whatever you expect them to do. If you don't know how to do it correctly, how will you know if they are? If you don't know what they do, how can you properly screen and evaluate prospective employees? And remember, everything which emanates from your office makes a statement about who you are, your level of professionalism, attention to your clients, and general quality of your work. If the work product is sloppy, the people who see it will assume your lawyering is, too.

There's another reason you need to know everything your staff does. One of these days, they or their kid will be sick and you'll have to do it yourself to meet a deadline.

NEVER blame your staff for your own screw up

I hate it when lawyers do this. It's offensive and unprofessional. The fact is that none of us is perfect, and you'll get a lot more respect if you own up to your mistake, do everything under the sun to make it right, and see that it doesn't happen again.

There's a corollary to this. What if it really *was* your secretary who screwed up? The classy answer is that you still don't publicly blame them. After all, *you're* the one who is in charge and who is ultimately responsible for the quality of the work your office produces. Everyone knows that, so to continually blame the staff creates the impression that you can't find or keep good staff or that you don't know how to supervise them. Either way, you lose 10 points.

The correct statement, regardless of who screwed up is, "I take full responsibility, Your Honor. This matter slipped through the cracks at my office (or whatever else happened). I assure you it won't happen again." And then take it up privately with your staff person to see that it doesn't. You'll get a lot more respect from all concerned.

Share the windfall

When you collect a big fee, share it with your staff. Even a small bonus reminds your staff that it took a team effort to get the fee, and that you appreciate their contribution. After all, they saw the mail when the check came in and know that you didn't earn it alone. I used to like to surprise my staff with small bonuses now and then. They never knew when they would open their paycheck and it would be there. They loved it when a few hundred dollars appeared without notice on the paystub. It reinforces the fact that you respect their contributions and builds loyalty.

Do your own work in a timely manner

Don't abuse them by doing everything at the last minute and expecting them to stay late to complete a project because you didn't do it in a timely manner yourself. This is the quickest way to lose good staff and goes back to treating them with respect. Procrastination on your part doesn't create an emergency on theirs. This is even more unforgivable if they've been nagging you to dictate the damn motion for weeks and you put it off until the day it has to be filed to deal with it. And what if *that's* the day their kid is sick and they have to go pick him up at school?

One of the partners in my old firm was notorious for calling his legal assistant five minutes before quitting time (he was *never* in the office then) and giving her two additional "rush" assignments that had to be done before she left. Don't do this. You will lose the staff you have, and pretty soon, you won't be able to get anyone competent to respond to your want ad. Word gets around in the legal community, staff talk to each other all the time, and you'll get the reputation you deserve. They'll recognize your phone number in the ad, and you will be doomed to an endless parade of incompetent slugs.

If you do your share of the work on time, so can they, and you'll both have some slack to deal with the inevitable unforeseen emergencies that go with the practice of family law.

With an extremely busy family law litigation practice, I didn't ask staff to work late or on a weekend more than four or five times in twenty five years. That meant that in the rare emergencies, they were happy to oblige. They also knew it was a true emergency and not occasioned by my procrastination. When it did happen, I took care to make the time up to them by giving them an afternoon off (at *their* convenience, and not just on a day when my own workload was light). I might even give them a gift certificate at their favorite store so they could go shopping on the time off. It did wonders for morale.

And colleagues wondered why they could never hire my superb staff away from me, no matter how hard they tried...

Remember that you can learn from your staff

You went to law school and they didn't. That being said, experienced staff people know many things that you need to know and weren't taught in law school. You may have gotten all sorts of academic awards, but probably don't know how to dictate a clear pleading or how to put your paperwork in a form the court clerks won't reject, or what information is necessary to a declaration and what is redundant. What may seem a simple clerical function to you may in fact be complicated. Proofs of service are a good case in point. They seem easy, but are extremely technical, and an entire case can be won or lost based on how carefully they are done. Never underestimate the importance of good staff work.

I was fortunate that in my first year, a very experienced legal assistant sat right outside my office door. She didn't work for me, of course. My firm would never have "wasted" such a talented employee on a new attorney. On more than one occasion, she heard me dictating something in my office and realized I was doing it wrong. She came in, closed the door, and gently told me how to do it right. I was tremendously grateful.

Then, the following year, I was blessed with the best legal assistant in the business. It was from her that I learned how to document a file, the importance of treating court personnel well, client relations, and all the other things which are required to make things happen in the real world. She was my true mentor in the nuts and bolts of practice, and remains my dear friend to this day.

Really smart law firms assign the best legal assistants to the newest lawyers for the first couple of years. This prevents the formation of bad work habits and pays in spades in later years.

They have a life, too

Be flexible with your staff and they will be with you. While you all try to compartmentalize the work part into "work hours," it isn't always that simple. They have kids, doctor's appointments, and other commitments.

Flexibility enables you not only to work the inevitable emergencies into your schedule, but to accommodate *their* emergencies as well. Don't let them abuse you and don't abuse them, either. If they know that you'll accommodate doctor or other appointments, especially if you get lots of advance notice, they'll be less likely to call in sick because that's the only way they can get their kid to the orthodontist. Sick calls are by definition last minute and leave no time for planning. Better that the orthodontia appointment has been on your calendar for two weeks and you know you'll be answering your own phone for an hour or two that day, instead of losing a whole day without notice.

I found that one of the beauties of working part time (and making my staff part time as well) was that if they weren't working Friday afternoons, or some other regularly scheduled time, they could schedule their personal appointments during that time, thus minimizing the disruption of the office. And if there were true emergencies, there was a ready-made time slot to get the work out.

What if you have no control over staff?

If you work for a firm, you'll probably be assigned a staff person whom you may or may not like. That's the way it is.

This can be particularly hard for new lawyers. As I've said, it is possible to learn from your staff. After all, they've probably been at this a lot longer than you. However, there are some things you should watch out for.

What if the staff treats you like the new kid on the block?

Well, the truth is, you are. You may know lots of law. Most of it was learned solely for the purpose of passing the bar and is totally irrelevant to what you are doing now. Now it is time to learn how to *practice* law. The staff has probably been doing this for years and knows the ins and outs of the practical side.

The fact is that a good legal assistant can save your butt. Be nice to them, courteous and professional, and expect the same from them. Learn whatever they can teach you about how to organize files, prepare paperwork, get it filed and served, and all the practicalities required to make things happen. If you do it right, you'll earn their respect soon enough.

That being said, don't let a staff person be condescending to you. Treat them with respect, and expect the same from them. If you allow a staff person to treat you disrespectfully, you'll have staff problems forever.

The Office Manager from Hell

The Office Manager from Hell exists. Sometimes he has your boss's ear. This is a pretty common situation. Sometimes it's because the office manager resents anyone else challenging what he perceives to be his authority. Sometimes he resents the fact that some upstart with a law school degree is trying to get ahead of him in the pecking order.

The only defense I know to this one is to be courteous and professional at all times and be sure your file is papered so that it demonstrates the competent work you are doing. And *don't* get involved in office politics if this is the agenda. Right now, the office manager is probably more valuable to your boss than you are. Focus on doing a stellar job while you're deciding whether life is too short to put up with the crap and move on to another firm or out on your own.

Eight

Opposing Counsel

What about opposing counsel?

It's important to have professional relationships with opposing counsel. You'll be coming up against the same people again and again throughout your career, long after this client is gone. Some of them will become close friends, at which point you will probably stop taking cases against each other.

That being said, your responsibility is to your client. *Never* put your own client down to curry favor with opposing counsel.

Where's the line between collegiality and caving in? It's always more pleasant to deal with someone you can get along with, who doesn't take the client's conflict personally, who doesn't exacerbate the situation. You want to have a good working relationship with opposing counsel. However, the legitimate interests of the client should never be sacrificed to maintaining the relationship. This is business, not a popularity contest. Always do your professional best.

Opposing counsel is the enemy, right?

Look at opposing counsel as someone who is a co-problem-solver, not the enemy. Neither of you created your clients' problem. The clients did that all by themselves before they consulted either of you. If you approach opposing counsel with the expectation that you can work together to solve the problem, you are more likely to get cooperation. Some of them will be jerks, but most simply want to find a solution that works for both sides, and be paid for it. You'll figure out which is which soon enough.

It's important not to personalize disagreements with the opposing attorney.. Not only will your life be more pleasant and your practice more successful, but there's another reason. You never know what is going on on the other side of the case and of course, your opponent can't (and shouldn't) tell you. If he is acting uncharacteristically pugnacious, there's probably something else driving it that you are unaware of.

I learned this early from an older lawyer. My new client had just been served with divorce papers. After hearing his side of the story, I called opposing counsel and commenced the rant that I thought was expected of me as an advocate. After listening for a few minutes he asked "Sue, why are you taking this so personally? This is about them, not us." One of many lessons I've never forgotten.

Don't take it personally, and leave it at the office.

Demonizing the other side

Some attorneys gear up for court by demonizing either the opposing party or attorney because that's the only way they can get up for the fight. Your client will likely demonize the other party or attorney. It isn't helpful if you do so as well. Demonizing the other side may help them get motivated for the battle, if that's what it takes, but it also makes it more likely that battle will be the inevitable result. If you adopt this style, you lose all objectivity and make a reasonable settlement infinitely harder to achieve, all to your personal stress and the detriment of your client.

What goes around comes around

If your opponent can't make the hearing and you tell her you'll appear and request a continuance, do it. If you proceed *in absentia*, you will have made an enemy for your professional life, and one who will tell the story to any colleague who will listen. Also, you will be exposing your client to the cost of setting aside the order and potentially exposing yourself to sanctions. Always play it straight. If you double-cross an opponent, he'll tell his colleagues and you'll be paying for it for years. What goes around comes around, and your opponent will have lots of opportunities in the future to retaliate in spades. And anyone to whom he told the story will assume you are a jerk and treat you accordingly.

Never complain about your own client to opposing counsel

I know I've said this before, but it bears repeating. If you have a problem client, the other side probably knows it. It's unprofessional, but far too many lawyers complain about their clients, not only to opposing counsel, but in chambers conferences with the judge.

The wages of "war stories"

Don't discuss other cases with opposing counsel. Attorneys love to tell war stories. Be careful what you say to opposing counsel. Not only is it a breach of confidentiality, it's also dumb. You're telling them a lot about yourself each time you do it. Do you really want them to have that much information about you? I've had more than one attorney tell me a war story at court which he thought reflected favorably on him and his brilliance, only to leave me shaking my head in disbelief when I got to my car.

There's another reason not to do this: You don't know who is friends with whom as you are gleefully describing the doofus attorney or client on the other side of the story. For all you know, the person on the next bench is the doofus' best friend.

What to do about "he said/she said" letters

Clients love these. The other side sends an inflammatory letter, and your client wants an even more incendiary reply. These exchanges are rarely productive, polarize the case, and burn precious litigation dollars which are better spent on substantive matters. When possible, take the high road. "My client takes great exception to the inaccurate accusations contained in your letter of the 12th. Let me assure you that your client's assessment of the facts is in error. Rather than respond in kind, I think it would be more productive to direct our attention to ways in which the situation can be resolved. Our proposal is...."

A good friend of mine is fond of saying that the only certain result of a pissing contest is that both participants have wet shoes.

The importance of professional courtesies

It happens all the time. You get a call from opposing counsel asking for a continuance. Remember, you'll have an emergency or calendar conflict sometime, too. Make sure your client isn't prejudiced by granting the courtesy. Don't let your client instruct you not to grant a benign, legitimate courtesy that doesn't adversely impact him. Sometimes they insist because they think the other side is the enemy and you should take every tactical advantage possible. If you adopt this as a habit, it will come back to bite you.

I learned this the hard way. A few months after I was admitted to the bar I was sent to cover a hearing for the partner I worked for. The other attorney didn't show, and his office called to say that he was sick. I called my boss and asked what I should do. He told me I should ask for monetary sanctions for my time in attending the hearing, which the judge granted. I promptly got a check in the mail from my opponent, but by that time I had figured out that what my boss had told me to do didn't feel right. I sent the check back to the opposing attorney by return mail with an apology. When I next saw my opponent, he was still angry and reminded me that someday I was going to get sick, too, and we had lots of cases against his office. Just because you *can* take advantage of an opponent doesn't mean you *should*.

And if an opponent always asks for courtesies but doesn't reciprocate, cross him off your list; it isn't a professional courtesy if he's not professional.

What to do with opposing counsel who tries to bully or intimidate you

When you are new, some will try. Sometimes it's obvious. Those are easy to deal with. Simply tell them that you will treat them professionally and expect to be treated the same. If they can't carry on a civil conversation, then perhaps you should be communicating by letter or email instead. If you let them get away with it, they will own you. Don't respond in kind; just remain professional, even if it takes everything you can muster to pull it off.

Sometimes the intimidation is more subtle. When I was a young lawyer, I frequently had cases against a particular old timer. This guy had been around since dirt was invented and was a bright, though extremely lazy lawyer. Every time we talked, he would tell me war stories about the old days (when I was still in preschool), referring to long-retired judges by their first names and generally rubbing my nose in the fact that I was a newbie. One day we were waiting for the judge to take the bench so we could start our hearing and he was doing his usual number. I finally had enough and asked him with mild curiosity in mid-sentence "Does this really work?" That brought him up short, and I followed up by saying matter of factly, "I'm just curious...I assume it must work with *some* young lawyers or you wouldn't keep doing it." He never did it again. At least, not with me.

How to know when life is just too short to deal with a particular opponent

Trust me. You'll know. There are some real jerks out there. Some people think that being a jerk is part of being a good advocate. It isn't. You'll probably have to get burned several times before you learn who these people are, or have a busy enough practice that you can afford to turn away cases where they are representing the other side.

What if he substitutes into a case you're already handling? You may be stuck. You can't abandon a client, and sometimes the other side hired the jerk for the express purpose of getting you off the case. And if you know before taking the case that the Jerk from Hell is on the other side, either refer it out or triple your retainer. You'll earn it.[14]

---

14 There's lots more detail about this dynamic in my book *How to Avoid the Divorce from Hell (and dance together at your daughter's wedding)* Third Edition, 2016, at Chapter 13, "What Happens When Your Spouse Hires the Lawyer from Hell." You can get it at amazon.com.

Nine

Always be courteous and professional

This seems to me like a no-brainer, so I'm constantly astounded at the people who try to bully clerks and are rude and argumentative with judges. Most judges take themselves and their position very seriously, and you denigrate them at your (and your client's) peril. Stridency is a poor substitute for a well-reasoned argument and judges hate it.

Likewise, never be a brown nose. Some judges may like it, but it won't help you when it comes time to make a ruling. The good judges will resent it because it implies that they would rule in your favor because you flatter them rather than because they are good judges who make thoughtful decisions.

Why it is important to thank the judge who just handed you a part of your anatomy

It's a matter of courtesy to say, "Thank you, Your Honor," at the end of a court proceeding. And if it sticks in your throat, remember that you are showing respect to the office, not necessarily the individual judge who happened to score a black robe through generous political contributions or a lucky election.

Corollary: Never thank a judge for a specific ruling in your favor. It implies he did it because he liked you and not because it was the right thing to do, and most judges will be mightily insulted.

Promises, Promises

Never make a representation to a judge that you can't prove. If you tell a judge that something is true, make sure it is. They'll never forgive being led down the primrose path, and the next time will probably doubt you, even if you're telling the truth and have ironclad proof.

Also, sometimes your client will lie to you. I know you're shocked to hear this, but it happens. Sometimes it's because his perception of what really happened is clouded by wishful thinking or subjective interpretation. Sometimes he really doesn't know and is speculating. And sometimes he's flat lying to you. When in doubt and the judge asks for your side of the story, the safe answer is "My client advises me," not, "I can prove...."

Who is making the decision, anyway?

A common beginner mistake in court is to engage in a dialogue with opposing counsel. Always address the judge or the witness in court, not opposing counsel. You aren't going to change your opponent's mind, but you might change the judge's. Directing your comments to the judge is a matter of simple courtesy. It also makes for a clean record. And don't talk over opposing counsel. Wait for them to finish before speaking up, and if they aren't letting you get a word in edgewise, ask the judge to protect your rebuttal time. If you're going to take something up on appeal, the record will be a mess if it is filled with attorneys talking over each other. After all, isn't the purpose of making a record to have an intelligible report of what actually went on?

Judges hate it when you bicker with or interrupt opposing counsel. Your client may love it, but it is unprofessional and dilutes your effectiveness.

And it goes without saying, *never* argue with the judge.

How to read the judge and what to do when you're losing him

Always watch the judge's demeanor and body language as your case is proceeding. He may not be giving anything away in facial expression, or verbally, but you can pick up a lot of signals. You'll get even better at this if you spend some time in the back of the courtroom watching other people try cases in front of the judge. It's easier to watch the judge closely when you're not cross examining a witness while your client tries to whisper in your ear. With practice, you'll learn to see if a particular judge reacts favorably or unfavorably to a particular tactic.

When the judge clearly isn't paying attention to what you are saying, stop talking. If the bailiff has approached the bench to give the judge a message just as you're about to hammer home the key evidence in your case, shut up until you have her attention or she signals you to proceed. And if the bailiff approaches the judge while your opponent is making *his* key points, keep your mouth shut and let it happen.

I remember concluding a hearing and seeing the judge stack up the files neatly on the bench. He put the exhibits on top of the files, his legal pad and calculator on top of that, and pens on top of all. The clear message was that he had heard all he needed to know, and had already made his decision. I made four quick points in closing argument, taking less than one minute. My opponent chose this time to drone on and on, laboriously revisiting the trial testimony. It turns out that I prevailed, but that isn't the point. Even if I was losing, the signal from the court was so clear that I would not have changed his mind by repeating what the witnesses and I had already said. The client may need to hear a closing argument, but if you get a signal like this from the judge, make it short and sweet.

When I was first in practice, I appeared before a law and motion judge who read the files carefully before taking the bench. He would point to one attorney and say "You're behind. Start talking." If I was the one pointed at, I knew I had a real sales job to change his mind. That's not the point of the story, however. Being a newbie, I didn't know that meant that I should shut up if I was ahead. After the other attorney had finished, I couldn't resist responding, which resulted in the judge turning to me and saying "You were ahead before, but you've raised another issue." Pretty soon, I was the one behind the eight ball, and solely because I didn't know when to keep my mouth shut.

How to get on the judge's blacklist

- Arrive unprepared.
- In the middle of a hearing, make everybody wait while you dig through your files to find the exhibit you want to use to question the witness. If your evidence isn't neatly organized, in the probable order you intend to use it, and pre-marked, don't presume to call yourself a trial lawyer.
- Talk over or interrupt the judge. I guarantee that if you do this, the court reporter will take down what the judge is saying rather than what you are saying, and the record won't reflect what you think it does. And besides, it's just rude.
- Always run over your time estimate.
- Make meaningless objections to harmless evidence just to prove you know the rules.
- Be condescending. Yes, there will be judges who are not as bright as you are, or don't know anything about the field of law they've been assigned to (later, of course; you don't know anything yet, but you will). They know when you are condescending, and resent it.
- Fumble over your questions, making it clear that you don't know what evidence you intend to elicit and haven't thought through how you intend to get it in.

- Ask the same question repeatedly, hoping to get a different answer. You won't and the judge will resent the waste of valuable court time.
- Fill your pleadings with irrelevant information and inflammatory accusations. This isn't good lawyering; it wastes the judge's time, and pretty soon she'll stop reading what you write, assuming that it is your usual drivel.
- Try to make up for a weak case with histrionics.
- Argue with opposing counsel rather than addressing the judge.
- Wait until you get to court to start talking to your client or opposing counsel about the case, keeping everyone else waiting.
- Lie to her.
- Waste her time.
- Whine.

When it's ok to ask to talk with the judge at the conclusion of a case and how to do it

Of course, it is obvious that you can't have *ex parte* conversations with a judge during the pendency of a case. However, there are times when it is appropriate to talk to the judge after the case is concluded and you are sure no additional issues on this case will be raised before this judge.

Early in my career, I was fortunate enough to appear before some stellar judges. If I felt a judge was kindly and not likely to throw me out of chambers, I would approach the judge a week or so after the conclusion of a case I had tried. I would ask the bailiff or clerk for a few minutes of the judge's time and would make good use of it. I would ask him (and they were *all* him in those days) what I could change that would improve the effectiveness of my presentation and what (if anything) he thought I did well. I didn't spend more than a few minutes with him and thanked him for his comments.

Of course, I did *not* discuss the facts of the case with the judge. That would be a breach of ethics. If you're going to ask her advice, keep your questions limited to trial techniques, how you could have presented your evidence more effectively and the like, *never* the substance of the case. And keep it short. Their time is very limited.

How to handle the judge who tries to bully you into sacrificing your client

Judges are under tremendous pressure to dispose of cases. Most of them do a yeoman's job of this under very trying conditions. A few will try to bully you into sacrificing your client's legitimate claims in the interests of moving the calendar along. Sometimes they do it because their calendars are so full they don't have time to hear the case. Sometimes they do it because they're lazy and would rather pressure you into a settlement than to have to go to the trouble of making a decision themselves.[15] Sometimes they are so afraid of getting reversed on appeal that they avoid making decisions at all. I've known a few of these.

So, what do you do? We all want the judges to like us. Also, clients come and go, and sometimes the judge is forever. On the other hand, the judge doesn't sue you. Your client might. The fact is that your ultimate responsibility is to the client, not the judge.

If you feel the judge is moving too fast or pressuring you to accept a settlement which is not in your client's interests, be calm and professional, but steadfast. "Your Honor, my client is entitled to be heard on this issue, I believe he has a valid claim, and I am ethically required to present it. I believe I would be committing malpractice to do otherwise." Don't argue, don't whine, and don't imply you are doing it just to placate your client. When phrased in this way, most judges will find it hard to say no.

---

15 I've always been baffled why someone who doesn't like making decisions wants to be a judge, but there you have it. It happens. I've known several.

What about the judge's staff?

It goes without saying that you need them more than they need you. If you're rude or pushy now, you might get what you want this time, but the next time you send them an order to be signed, it will go to the bottom of the pile. Be professional and courteous, and don't do things that make their job harder. Of course, some of them don't work a lick, but never let on that you know that. Let them complain to you about how overworked they are. And remember that most of them really are. Show that you appreciate what they do for you, whether it is finding your order in the judge's signature pile and moving it to the top, or chasing down the court file you need to read. And don't bad mouth opposing counsel. You never know who they consider their friend.

The court staff can make your life either prodigiously easier or a nightmare of lost paperwork. They are also a terrific source of referrals. When their friends need a lawyer, they are likely to be asked for a referral. If they think you are good, or know that the judge they work for thinks so, this can be a great boost to building a practice. Don't blow it by letting your ego trump courtesy and common sense.

Ten

KILLING TREES: HOW TO DO GOOD PAPERWORK

Whether it is hand carried, faxed, or e-filed, good paperwork is a lawyer's stock in trade. Lots of lawyers haven't a clue how to write effectively. Here are a few of the basics:

We aren't paid by the word any more

Be clear and succinct. There's no reward for writing the longest brief. You may think you are impressing your client, opponent and the court with how brilliant you are. Most judges don't have time to read long, turgid briefs. If your argument flows crisply, relates back to the facts of the case, and quickly builds toward the conclusion you want the judge to reach, it's more likely to be read and followed. If you didn't get a first rate legal writing class in law school, this is taught multiple times at every State Bar annual meeting. You can get it online. There's no excuse not to.

A leads to B leads to C leads to success

Make your conclusion flow from the facts and the analysis. This seems pretty obvious, but too many attorneys forget that a legal argument is designed to move from A to B to C to D to whatever conclusion you want the judge to reach. At best, when you do this right, you make D look like the only tenable conclusion. Don't do it in a hurry and forget to make the leap from B to C. State the facts, cite the law, and write a clear analysis of why they require the result you want.

And if you find yourself using the word "clearly" every other paragraph in your brief, it isn't. That's an almost universal red flag of a weak argument. If it's really that clear, you won't need to tell the judge so.

All arguments aren't created equal

Put your strongest arguments first and eliminate your weakest arguments. I learned this writing for a judge who was famous for only reading the first page or two of any brief. I got quite good at getting enough information on that page to give him a good flavor of the case and, on a good day, pique his interest to read the rest. Even if you have a judge who reads every word, it's good practice.

There is no rule that says you have to make every possible argument which *might* support your case. In fact, all that does is dilute your case. I used to write briefs starting with the strongest arguments, moving to the weakest, and the conclusion. Before putting the brief in final form, I would reevaluate to make sure the arguments were still in the right order, especially at the beginning, and I would change the order of presentation to make it flow more smoothly. Then I would go back and delete the weakest argument.

Eliminate extraneous facts

Do this even if your client really, really wants the court record to reflect what a schmuck the other party is. If the facts aren't relevant to the issue, leave them out. All they'll do is incite the other side, who will be compelled to respond in kind and distract the judge from the conclusion you're trying to get him to reach.

Always check your authorities

I know they taught you this one in law school. It still bears repeating. Mislead a judge once, and he'll never forget. We all hate to be made to look stupid, and judges simply don't have the time to check your sources and Shepardize your cases. And if there's a killer case which makes your issue a slam dunk, provide the judge with a copy along with your brief. She may not have time to track it down herself.

How to prepare exhibits the judge will love

Compilation exhibits can make or break a case. Make them clear and succinct. Leave lots of white space on your exhibit, especially on the front page. You want *your* exhibit to be the one the judge takes notes on, not your opponent's.

If the information is complicated, do a summary cover sheet which is as simple as possible and attach the backup data, marking, numbering or tabbing it for easy reference. That way the judge can turn quickly to the backup and see where you got a particular figure or conclusion. Incidentally, it's well worth the cost of index tabs and exhibit labels when you're in the middle of trial and need to get your evidence admitted without fumbling.

In the summary, refer back to the source of the specific evidence on which it is based, and label it accurately so the judge can easily flip back and verify that the bank statement really does say what you say it does. You'll lose him if he has to go through reams of irrelevant data to find the one fact he's looking for. He simply won't have time to do it and you'll lose the opportunity to make your point.

Yes, it takes more time to do it right, and you can't leave it to the last minute, as you probably have to provide it to opposing counsel prior to trial. Some attorneys don't like to do this because they're afraid they will tip their hand to opposing counsel. Of course, that is the risk. But when all is said and done, it's the judge who makes the decision, and I'd rather make it easy for him to rule in my favor than to play hide the ball with my opponent, only to find I've hidden the ball from the judge as well.

Never put dangerous or confidential facts in a public record

Seems pretty obvious, but this rule is probably honored more in the breach than the observance. It stands to reason that the IRS is looking, so why on earth would you file a declaration saying the parties have filed fraudulent (joint) tax returns for years? When a client wanted me to point out the fact that the other spouse has been committing tax fraud for years, my response always was, "Signed the joint return, did you?" and then watch for realization to dawn. If it didn't dawn, I'd start talking about joint and several liability, accessory to a crime and the like. If that didn't work, I'd point out to them that there are rewards for people who report tax fraud, and someone in the clerk's office or sitting in the back of the courtroom might think this is a great opportunity to score a quick ten percent.

Sometimes the facts seem innocuous, but aren't. Never put your client's social security number in a public record, and *never* attach the Schedule C or any other part of the tax return to a pleading filed with the court without redacting sensitive information. When referring to loans and credit cards, use only the last few digits and omit or redact (lawyer-speak for black out) the others.[16] In this era of identity theft and court files available online, this is just common sense.

Likewise, be careful about inserting information which would harm the client's children if they saw it. The kids may find information which they have no business seeing, just because it is a public record. Some kids are curious enough to look up their parent's divorce records. Some people are nosy and

---

16 Incidentally, if you are redacting numbers from a document to be used in evidence or filed with the court, don't just black them out and use that for the original. Always keep the original document complete and unmarked. Make a copy and redact *that one*. Then make the photocopies you are actually going to use from the redacted one. Otherwise, it is likely that the blacked out information is still legible when held up to the light.

cruel enough to check out their neighbor's divorce file and share the juicy parts at the block party. Public court records are becoming internet accessible, for crying out loud, so don't take the chance.

If the facts need to be pled and there's no way around it, ask for an order sealing the file and for a closed hearing.

Review spells success

Prepare your briefs early enough so you have time to fine tune them before the filing deadline. The quality will improve immensely with even a single review and revision. You may find that the argument which sounded so good in your head doesn't translate well to paper. If you review it in advance, you have time to think about a better or more persuasive way to say it, or other arguments which might be more effective. Sometimes the mere act of revisiting your work with a clear head will cause you to see the killer argument which you had completely overlooked.

And of course, this relates back to client relations: if your client has to sign it, write it early. Give them a chance to review or correct it. After all, your client is busy, too. They need uninterrupted time to review the document to be sure it is correct before they sign it. They may have to wait until the after the kids are in bed, or after they return from an important business trip. Giving them lead time to consider carefully whatever they are signing is a critical component of client relations. It tells them that you care about the completeness and accuracy of their legal document. It confirms your respect for the fact that their legal issue deserves serious attention, both from them and from you, and it demonstrates your respect for their own time commitments. All of these things spell good client relations.

Eleven

Rule #1: It doesn't matter how many hours you bill

This goes entirely against the conventional wisdom of traditional law practice management. But the fact is that the only relevant statistic is how many dollars you *collect,* not how many hours you bill.

This is another one of those rules which seems obvious when you think about it, but which most lawyers don't get. Billable hours create accounts receivable. Collected dollars create bank deposits. Never confuse the two. And if you get paid for *all* of the time you work instead of only part of it, you don't have to work as many hours to make a good living, do you?

What if you work for a firm which sets a quota for billable hours?

Though many if not most law firms do it, I think giving inexperienced lawyers a mandatory quota for billable hours is a horrible business practice. New lawyers haven't learned their craft yet. A mandatory quota for billable hours encourages them to be inefficient with their time so that they can meet their quota, at precisely the time when they should be learning efficiency and good work habits. It encourages them to do "make work" to meet the quota, which translates directly into higher accounts receivable, much of which never gets paid. Most law firms will write off the unreasonably high bill which results, but then blame the associate, rather than their own lousy business practices and priorities which led to a predictable result.

It also illustrates the disconnect in our profession that there's some relation between mere hours worked and professional performance.

My suggestion is to concentrate on dollars collected rather than hours billed. Incidentally, I've rarely seen a young associate who is good at collection. This is a skill you should be learning since you may well be working for yourself at some time and will need to know how to do it.

If you're in this position, concentrate on collecting for the time you bill. Your boss will love it, because it is so rare. And if you are criticized about the number of hours you bill, you'll have an answer because you can remind him that mere billable hours don't go into his pocket, whereas collected ones do.

How to bill

Learn to record all your time working on a case. You may reduce it later, but if you don't record it as you do it, how do you know how much time a particular task should have taken? You will probably be writing off a fair bit of time as you are learning. So be it. Practice doing great work, and on learning good work habits. You'll be able to work more efficiently in the future.

Use a good timekeeping program, keep it minimized on your computer, and start the timer when you take the phone call, dictate the letter, start the consultation, etc. Enter your time yourself rather than keeping a paper timesheet which you have to pay someone else to input into the billing system. Record your court time as soon as you walk back into the office. Never wait to fill out timesheets or time entries until the end of the day, or, God forbid, the end of the week. You'll *never* reconstruct all of the time.

When breaking for lunch, add up the time you billed so far that day. If it isn't as much as you think you put in, take a couple of minutes to think back over your morning and recall other things you did which you forgot to record. It's a lot easier to pick up those phone calls and memos within a few hours than to try to do so at the end of the day. Also, before leaving the office for the day, take a moment to review the time you've recorded to see if there is something you forgot to enter. You won't remember it tomorrow, or when you're reviewing your bills before sending them out.

Learn to be efficient with your time. Your clients will love it, and you'll have less to answer for later.[17] We all think we're selling hours to our clients. In fact, what they are buying is results. They'll love it if they compare your bill to opposing counsel's bill presented at the fee hearing and see that you did the same work in significantly less time. And, unlike other areas of the law, in family law these records routinely become available to the other side to scrutinize and compare.

Although it goes without saying, never bill for more time than you actually spent.[18] Do not pad your hours. Clients will know and resent it. Ours is the only kind of practice where our bills not only become part of the court record when attached to a fee motion, but our clients routinely compare their lawyer's bills with those of the opposing side. How will you explain it to your

---

17 You never know when this will come back to you. I was in trial waiting for the judge to come back from lunch to start the afternoon session when my client went into the ladies room. She was gone so long I began to be concerned. When she came out, she had a big grin on her face. She had struck up a conversation with a friendly stranger who asked her why she was there and, after finding out it was a divorce, who her lawyer was. It turns out the friendly stranger was a former client of mine, a successful business woman, who was there to testify on a business matter. She told my client that I had represented her as well and that she was in very good hands. Then she said that she loved the fact that I was extremely efficient and did things in a third of the time her ex-husband's lawyer billed. She had never told *me* that, but volunteered it to my client.

18 The exception to this, discussed elsewhere, is time billed to recoup the cost of drafting complex forms such as marital settlement or prenuptial agreements which are used and updated time after time.

client if you billed .5 hours for a phone call with opposing counsel, and *he* billed .2 hours, including the memo he dictated afterward?

Clients like to see where their legal dollars are going. Put detailed descriptions of what you have done on your bill. When in doubt, insert more detail rather than less. You can always redact the sensitive detail if you have to attach the bill to a fee motion. You should do this anyway if you are required to disclose billing records to prevent your work product or other confidential information from appearing in a public record.

A corollary is to examine your opponent's bills when you have the opportunity (on your own time if necessary) to see what billing techniques they use and if they are accurate and effective. Pretend you are on the receiving end of the bill and make a note of which techniques are off-putting and which clearly describe the services rendered in a way which reinforces their reasonableness. Remember, the idea is to send a bill which clearly demonstrates what you did for the client, so that he recognizes the benefit he got for the services and is more likely to pay for them.

I'm not a fan of minimum charges for simple tasks. If your firm policy is that a letter is a mandatory 15 minutes (or, worse, 30 minutes, as it is in some firms!) and you bill that much time for the stock letter that says "Enclosed is a copy of today's correspondence from opposing counsel. Please call after you have reviewed it so we can discuss our response," the client is going to feel screwed. A better timesheet entry is "review correspondence from attorney X and dictate correspondence to client re same." And bill only for the actual time spent. There are lots of things, such as research, drafting, trial preparation and the like which are much fuzzier, but I guarantee that a client who gets a big charge for what is obviously a simple letter will be unhappy, and will probably question you not only on that one, but the legitimate entries on your bill as well.

And when you're sending that stock transmittal letter asking the client to call after reviewing it, it is helpful if you add some suggestions for possible responses that she can think about before she calls.

When not to bill

Don't bill for your time performing purely clerical work. If you don't have staff and are doing your own work, adjust your time. That is built into the hourly rate for legal work.

You're brand new. Of course there is a learning curve. Presumably that is partly reflected by the fact that you charge a lower hourly rate than more experienced colleagues. When you're really educating yourself on an issue or procedure you haven't seen before, you may not want to bill for all your time.

Never bill for the time you spend fixing something you screwed up. This seems obvious, but I've seen people do it. There's no quicker way to sour client relations. If you made a mistake, fix it immediately and on your own time.

When to reduce a bill

If you know you spent too much time in relation to the product produced, it is better to reduce the bill up front than to wait until the client challenges it. And, except for the time you spend educating yourself, I think it is generally good client relations to let the client know that you reduced the bill, the amount of the reduction, and the reason. You wouldn't send a bill that says "Reduced by 10% because I don't know anything yet." But you might just mark it reduced, or add a note that indicates you believe in retrospect that it took more time than it should have. That sends several messages to your client: you reviewed the work personally and thought about the value of the service to the client. You carefully reviewed the billing detail and made a conscious decision to adjust it. You've demonstrated your efforts to be fair with them, which makes them want to be fair with you.

Sometimes it is good business to not charge for a specific service. If you decide to do this, put the service on your bill anyway with the words "no charge." It is a great client relations tool.

If your client is unhappy about a particular charge, it is sometimes a good practice to reduce it (that is, if you want to keep good relations with this client) than to steadfastly refuse and create hard feelings. Use your judgment on this one. If you feel strongly that the client received good value and is just trying to bully you into reducing your bill, that is the time to stand firm, or perhaps suggest that the client needs a different lawyer. The client who is just trying to squeeze you for a few bucks doesn't really want another lawyer, and will probably back down. The one who really is unreasonable may have an unrealistic idea of what it takes to turn out a quality product. That should be an opportunity for a sit-down where you explain all of the thought, research, analysis, and assembly which was necessary to present the product in an intelligible and persuasive manner to the judge.

Of course, if the client makes this his practice and is using it as a technique to get out of paying a legitimate and reasonable fee, don't let him get away with it. Better yet, start developing a strategy for getting out of the case. This client will never be satisfied and will likely take you to fee arbitration.

How to talk to a client about money

Never be embarrassed or apologetic about asking a client to pay your bill. They are expected to pay the grocery store and the dentist. If my veterinarian can expect payment at the time of service, why should I be embarrassed to ask that I be paid for my services in a reasonable time?

Be very matter of fact. There are several ways to do this:

"If you don't pay the bill, you are borrowing from me. I'm not set up to and can't afford to be a bank."

"I have overhead to meet. My rent and legal assistant and telephone still have to be paid, and it is unfair to my other clients to expect them to pay for the costs associated with the work my staff and I did on your case."

"I have to answer to my boss/partners if I don't carry my share of the overhead."

And my all time favorite:

"I always give your case my prompt attention; I expect my bill to receive the same prompt attention from you."[19]

Here's a technique which I found to be effective when a bill went un-paid in an ongoing case: At the end of a telephone call with your client, after you've addressed all their business, and have agreed on what they want you to do next, ask if you've covered everything on their list. When they assure you that you have, you can say "Now we need to talk about my list. My bill is now $_____, and it needs to get paid. When can I expect payment?" Be *very matter of fact,* neither apologetic nor accusatory, and then wait for the answer. Don't fill the silence, even if it is awkward. This works because they know they've just asked you to do a whole lot of ad-ditional work. It underscores the necessity of paying for prior work before asking for more, and reinforces the connection between your time and their money.

And, when the client says "You know my financial situation better than I do; you've seen the financial data and you *know* I'd pay you if I could," the answer to that is, "Maybe you can't afford me. Perhaps we need to limit my involvement in your case to the areas which are most important, or perhaps you can't afford an attorney at all." If they truly can't afford you, better to find that out while they only owe you a little rather than after they owe you a lot. And if they can only afford to pay you to do part of the case, that's the time to explore whether you should change your involvement to limited scope. A good way to broach the subject is to say "if you can't afford me, we should ex-plore the ways in which we can make the best use of your litigation budget."[20]

---

19 Of course, you can only say this if it is absolutely true. If you have been putting off the case and ignoring emails and phone calls, not paying your bill may be the way the client has chosen to get your attention back where it belongs.

20 Much more information about this is in my book *Unbundling Your Divorce: How to Find a Lawyer to Help You Help Yourself.* You can get it at amazon.com.

How not to do it

Don't get mad at them because, although you've been sending bills for months, you haven't mentioned it to them, and have never asked them for money. If *you* don't make your bill a priority, why should *they?*

Some people feel strongly that collections should be delegated to staff rather than done by the attorney. I did that when I didn't know anything about billing and client relations. However, I learned with experience that it isn't effective. While it is certainly easier to hide behind your office manager, and may be awkward to talk about money, it is also easier for the client to slough off the staff person. There is nothing to be embarrassed about expecting to be paid for your work. Presumably you are working hard, learning as fast as you can, and doing the best possible job you can. Your hourly rate most likely reflects your level of experience. You are entitled to be paid for your work. Also, if you can talk to your client about money while making eye contact, you can talk to them about anything. Since the number one client complaint is lack of effective communication, this is an important skill to develop.

The worst thing is to keep sending bills, and then get mad and write a nasty letter without ever discussing the issue directly with your client. I understand that it can be awkward to talk about money. Trust me, if you don't get the hang of it, you'll pay the price in uncollected accounts receivable. It isn't a bad idea to put a handwritten note on the bill asking when it is going to be paid. They will probably recognize your handwriting, and know that you've personally reviewed it.

Exercise some independent judgment. Although I had only been a lawyer a year or so, I should have realized that the client who wanted me to fight for the value of the meat in the freezer when he left the family home (because it was purchased with joint funds!) was not going to pay me for that fight.

If your client is living out of his truck, don't run up thousands of dollars in legal fees. Unless you're doing the case *pro bono* or for the experience, don't do it. I once had a client who was delegated to me by the partner I worked for.

Not only was I operating under the Associate Rule #1 to bill! bill! bill!, but I really liked her and believed in her case. I had neither experience, authority, nor objectivity. I should have seen that she wasn't going to be able to pay me, but I didn't.

I faithfully billed her month after month (or rather, the firm's bookkeeping department did) and she became embarrassed about the size of the bill and her inability to pay it. We never talked about money, because my instructions were to leave that to bookkeeping and concentrate on the law. At Christmas she gave me a personalized handmade Christmas ornament. I like to think of it as my "$20,000 ornament." It has hung on my Christmas tree for almost 40 years. I don't resent her for it. If that case had come along when I was running my own firm, I probably would still have taken it, and given it the best I had, because I truly did believe in her. I just would have known that it was *pro bono* and approached it accordingly.

"It's not the money; it's the principle"

Sooner or later, you will tell a client that the course of action they want you to take is not cost effective, and they will respond "It's not the money; it's the *principle*." When you hear these words, red flags should be popping up all over the place. This is a recipe for disaster because the client is admitting that he is litigating for emotional rather than practical reasons. After you've done the work and that emotional charge is translated into cold, hard, dollars that they have to pay *you*, they won't want to.

Always insist that your client quantify how much he is willing to pay for the principle and make him come up with a number. I would always start with something small and ask them "Would you pay $300 for it? $500? $1,000?" Then substitute something fun that the money might otherwise be used for, such as a nice vacation. If they persist, estimate how much you think it will cost to do the work, and make the client front the money. Put it in your trust account. Usually, this alone puts the "principle" in perspective.

If they still insist on going forward and you've got the money in your trust account, send the client a letter reminding them that you recommend against it, that it is a poor use of their funds and your time. You'll need a copy of this letter at the fee arbitration when they ultimately realize you were right and it really wasn't worth it.

Never underwrite *their* principle out of *your* pocket. You won't get paid.

How to be sure you get paid

Pay as you go is the only safe way. It keeps clients realistic. It's far too easy to run up huge fees on stupid issues if there's no expectation they will have to make immediate payment. Remember, their emotional investment in the case is probably clouding their judgment. If you're insisting on being paid as you go, fighting for the principle may look much less appealing. It also makes the client much more realistic about that "outrageous" settlement offer from the other side which they've just rejected.

We can rarely estimate the total cost of a legal matter at the beginning. That's why we bill by the hour. One way of staying on top of a case is to use what is called an "evergreen" retainer. That means that the client deposits a retainer in your trust account. When it drops below a predetermined level, they are expected to replenish it. If they can't, that is the time to talk about whether you should switch to limited scope or otherwise curtail your involvement to those aspects of the matter where your expertise is most essential. That keeps them realistic about the mounting cost of the case, and prevents the growth of a receivable which is truly unmanageable.

If you are working for yourself or have control over the billing cycle, it is a good practice to send bills out before the first of the month. I always sent my bills out no later than the 25th of the month, so they were in the client's hands on the first, which is when most people sit down to pay bills.

If you wait until the first of the month to send the bill, they won't receive it for a day or two, by which time they've probably already spent their money on other bills. As a result, they won't look at yours again until their next paycheck. That means you've guaranteed that you'll wait at least two weeks before payment, even if they pay "promptly." Also, another reason to do your own billing in house is so you can send the bill immediately after you've gotten the great result, while the client is still feeling appreciative of your work.

It is essential that you take credit cards. Most practitioners who start to accept credit cards report an immediate increase in collections of upwards of 30%. It isn't unprofessional. It is good business. Shop around to get the best rate, and don't assume that will be your own bank. You don't need to have the fancy NCR credit slips, either. Create your own half page form with all the information the credit card company needs. Copy it two to a page and cut them in half. Slip the half page form into the envelope with your bill and the return envelope, and you'll be amazed how many you get back by return mail. And always include a self addressed envelope to make it easy for them to return the credit card slip or check to you.

Review your accounts receivable list every month (I know, lawyers *hate* to do this because it reminds them how much of their life they've given away to something they may not get paid for.) Do it anyway. Not only will it remind you who is falling behind before they get so deep that they truly have no ability to pay, but it will also remind you which cases you haven't seen in a while which may need attention. If someone has fallen behind, that's the time to pick up the phone and talk to them about their plans for payment. It may not be a comfortable call, but it is necessary.

When to take it on faith

Occasionally, you have to trust a client to pay you later. When I was a young lawyer, I was once consulted by a man who couldn't raise my rather modest retainer (an amount which I won't mention because it sounds ridiculously low in today's dollars). I knew he had a house which would ultimately be sold and which had substantial equity. I really liked the guy, he had fallen on hard times, and my gut told me to trust him. I did the entire case on the come, and at the end, when the house sold, a part of me wondered what would happen. He was a very proud man, and told me he would be embarrassed if I put a demand into escrow to be paid by the title company, as he didn't want his wife to see that he hadn't paid me yet.

I struggled with letting him take all the funds from escrow rather than submitting a claim, but having trusted him that far, I decided to trust him one more day. The day after escrow closed, he came by my office and paid me in full. The amount then due was something like $2,871.99. He insisted on writing his check for $2,872 and was quite firm that the penny he received in change had to be extremely shiny. I didn't have one which he thought was shiny enough, so I had to go down the hall to find a staff member who had a brand new penny in her purse. A week later, he brought me a small piece of burl wood which he had sanded and finished and on which he had mounted the penny. He gave it to me as a reminder that some people are trustworthy. That was in 1981, and I am looking at it as I write this line. It has always been and will remain on my desk.[21]

On another occasion, I was consulted by a client I really connected with. Her prior attorney had done a lousy job on a very complex issue, she had no money for a retainer, and yet, if the earlier mistake could be fixed, she stood to receive a substantial property settlement on a very unusual set of facts. I frankly didn't think anyone else would take her, and believed that only someone as good as I was could pull off this very difficult case. She offered me her jewelry as security for her retainer. I really believed in her case, trusted her, and was reluctant to take the jewelry. However, it was important to her to feel that she was compensating me in some way for my faith in her. I ultimately

---

21 And incidentally, I've never taken a deed of trust on a client's house in lieu of retainer in my life. It just doesn't seem right or fair and puts me in an immediate conflict of interest with them. How would I feel evicting my own client from her house? I make them borrow it elsewhere, get it from the other side, make other arrangements, decline the case or, in the rare, extremely rare case, look at my penny (which is much less shiny with the passage of years) and take it on the come.

took the jewelry (which was worth a fraction of my usual retainer), and put it in my safe.

I assumed that the case was going to be *pro bono*, and knew I wasn't going to keep her jewelry at the end. The resulting legal bill was a large one, but I ultimately negotiated a very creative and favorable settlement with her husband's lawyer, with which she was thrilled. As soon as she got her money, she validated my faith in her by paying every penny, and I gave her jewelry back, as I always knew I was going to.

Make those cases few and far between. Do it only when your gut tells you this is a special client, and not just because he is whining to get you to underwrite his case. And sometimes they can't or won't pay you at the end. Assume at the beginning that these cases are *pro bono*; then you'll be pleasantly surprised when you get paid in full.

How to deal with the case that turns sour

It will happen. It's too late to get out because trial is approaching and it's too late for the client to obtain new counsel. You hate your client and she hates you.

As hard as it is, do your best to communicate directly with her, and paper your file. Make sure you have something in writing telling her that the law doesn't provide for the relief she's demanding you pursue. Make sure the tone of your communications is professional. Confirm every conversation in writing if possible. And put on the cleanest damn trial you can. DON'T settle this one on the courthouse steps. She'll just claim that she would have gotten more if you had only gone before the judge. Or worse, she'll say she settled under duress because you had lost confidence in her case and she had lost confidence in *you*. There are some cases which just have to be tried, because at least you'll have a court record which will demonstrate that you did a professional job. It's just too dangerous to settle this one, especially if it's under pressure at the courthouse.[22]

---

22 Ditto for the client whom you discover too late is a hopeless alcoholic or druggie. They may not be able to give informed consent to a settlement. In that case, you'll need to have a record to protect you.

If you do settle this one, make sure there is no time pressure and you've instructed your client to get a second opinion before signing on the dotted line. And make sure you have a CYA[23] letter which documents all the reasons why the settlement is in her best interests, citing all the weaknesses in the case which would have been exposed if it went to trial.

The clash between crusades and business

Sometimes there's a case you take because you really love the cause and want to make a difference. That's ok. That's why many of us went to law school in the first place. But now that you're in private practice, what does it mean in the real world?

If it's really a crusade, assume it's *pro bono* and be sure it's *your* crusade and not your client's. There's never any percentage in underwriting your client's crusade from your own pocket, and that's what you're doing if you're not insisting on getting paid as you go. You'll end up resenting them mightily, and the residual bad feelings may well poison your willingness the next time you are drawn to do a good deed.

If it's *your* crusade, then presumably you're operating from an agenda other than profit. Understand what your motivation is and how much of your own time you are willing to invest in it. Do it with your eyes open, and with a budget in mind which you are not willing to exceed. Otherwise, it will eat you alive.

What happens when you get burned on fees? (and you will)

When you get burned, you have a choice. You can blame the client and forever view everyone who comes through your office as a potential deadbeat. This will guarantee that you project a slightly hostile energy toward your potential clients and probably attract more of the same to you. Or, you can

---

23 Cover Your Anatomy

analyze the situation, figure out what you could have done differently and then treat it as the learning experience it was.

Take responsibility for your financial relations with your clients. I was once furious with a client who owed me $20,000 long after the case was over. I knew he could afford it and sent him bills for months, to no effect. I then found out he'd bought a new ski boat worth more than he owed me. I was livid for about half an hour until I realized that if *I* hadn't made my bill a priority, why should I have expected *him* to? What message was he drawing from the fact that I kept sending bills without follow up, other than that I didn't take it very seriously? I'd never had the conversations I should have had with him. I called him, worked out a payment schedule (since he'd already spent his ready cash on the boat, you see) and learned a valuable lesson.

How to stay out of fee arbitration

The best way to stay out of fee arbitration is to have clear communication with your client about the work you do, how you bill, and your expectations about how your bill is to be paid. Too many lawyers blow this one because they're afraid that if they confront this subject directly, the client will feel the lawyer isn't on the same team. It's business, folks.

Talk directly with your client about your fees, your expectations, and her responsibilities. After all, you're shouldering a great deal of responsibility for her case. There's nothing wrong with expecting her to shoulder responsibility for paying you.

And don't let them fall into the trap that "the other side will pay." In family law, we do sometimes have the ability to have the court order the opposing party to pay some part of our fees. However, it is essential that your own client be reminded as often as possible that she is primarily responsible for paying the bill. There are several reasons for this. One is that she may not want to hear it, so she'll "forget" that you told her. I have said it until I am blue in the face only to get to the end of the case and hear her say "I thought my husband was going to have to pay this." The most important reason, though, is that there's no more unreasonable client than the one who thinks he can litigate endlessly for free. If the client doesn't think he's going to be stuck for the bill, it is far too easy to litigate over minutiae until the bill is stratospheric.

Don't barter for fees or trade services. Not only is it illegal (unless the full value appears on your tax return), but it is bad client relations, and demeans the value of your work. If a client wants to pay you in cash, make sure that they know that you will adhere to the IRS mandatory reporting requirements to the letter. I was once consulted by a very slimy lawyer on his own child support matter. He was trying to skip on child support (charming guy). At the end of the consultation, he asked how much he owed me, and whether he should make the check to cash or to me (which told me worlds about how he did business). Don't ever fall for this one. I smiled sweetly and pointed out to him that any cash I received would all go into the same bank account and be fully reported for tax purposes.[24] I then showed him the door.

Spot potential problems early. If you think the client isn't using her legal dollar wisely, tell her so, and document your file. Don't wait until the amount due is out of hand to have these discussions. Always be matter of fact, never angry, apologetic or hurt because they didn't pay your bill.

And of course, the best way to stay out of fee arbitration is to get paid as you go. Very few clients who have paid their lawyers subsequently take them to fee arbitration. That is usually reserved for cases where the lawyer belatedly tries to collect a stale fee that the client doesn't want to pay. At best, fee arbitration gives them a chance to get the bill reduced or canceled, and at worst, buys them some time. Large receivables breed fee arbitrations. They also breed malpractice claims, for the same reasons.

---

24 There's another reason not to take cash fees or to make sure the client knows you will be reporting it for tax purposes if you do. If a case goes sour, you don't want your client to ever have anything to hold over your head. Engaging in tax fraud is a crime, and creating the impression that you might even *think* about it is incredibly stupid.

The deadbeat client

Though I've taken clients to fee arbitration, I've never sued a client for fees.

It's better to compromise your bill or work out a payment schedule, if you can do it. Fee arbitration is a last resort, and (some lawyers will disagree with me on this one) suing a client for fees is an invitation to a malpractice counter-suit, no matter how unfounded it may be. The purpose of the countersuit is to induce you to compromise your claim. Why not compromise it at the beginning and save yourself the grief and the increased malpractice insurance premiums which result from defending a lawsuit, even if it was without merit? It makes a lot more sense to reduce a bill to get immediate payment rather than take the chance of burning your deductible defending a malpractice suit, even a bogus one.

One effective way to do this is to send the client a letter offering to reduce the bill to a specific amount (say, by 10% to 20%) if they pay in a relatively short period of time. Tailor this to the case, the client's realistic ability to borrow, and the like. You may want to do it in stages, saying you'll reduce it by one amount if paid within 10 days, and by a lesser amount if paid within 30 days. This often induces the well intentioned client to go out and borrow the money. I found this technique particularly effective in October or November, accompanied by a letter stating "While conducting my year end file review, I note that your bill is $____ and ____ days overdue. I'd like to get this off my books by the end of the year." Quote a percentage discount you will accept if it is paid in full by a particular date. This technique is effective on several levels. It reinforces that you do regular reviews of your accounts receivable and are paying attention. It states a non-accusatory reason for asking for it now. You want clean books at the end of the year. You're not calling him a deadbeat. And he probably hasn't spent all his available credit on Christmas yet, so there may be some room for a cash advance on a credit card or from some other source. The worst time to do it is January, when the holiday bills are just coming home to roost. Or work out a payment schedule they can afford (and follow up to see that they adhere to it). When setting up a payment schedule, it's a good idea to confirm with a letter that states you're willing to waive interest if they keep to the schedule and if they don't, it all comes due. It's not as good as payment in full now, but it sure beats a poke in the eye....

How to win at fee arbitration

You will ultimately be taken to fee arbitration. Sometimes it's because the client is unhappy with the result of the case. Sometimes it's because you didn't step in and stop the client from using you and your office for emotional support. Sometimes it's because the client never intended to pay you at all. Sometimes it's because the other side was a jerk and unreasonably ran up your fees.

I only lost one fee arbitration, and learned the lesson in spades. I've told the story elsewhere, under client relations, but it bears repeating here, under billing. It was a very needy client in a difficult case the first year I was in practice. The opposing party was a lawyer, and his attorney was the Prime Jerk in the local family law bar, who fought every issue. It also wasn't my case. The partner for whom I worked delegated it to me so he wouldn't have to deal with the Prime Jerk or our own needy client. As a result, the client was constantly calling, dropped by almost every day to see me on some pretext, and I dutifully reported it on my timesheet as I was instructed to do[25].

She ultimately took us to fee arbitration (which, of course, my boss assigned *me* to defend). Her position was "It wasn't worth it." She was right. She was getting hand holding, not legal work. It *wasn't* worth it. And I'm the professional and should have told her so. Admittedly, I had been in practice only a few months and did what my boss told me. That's not the point. The point is that it *wasn't* worth it. I'm a lawyer, not a therapist, and I should have suggested that she go elsewhere for emotional support. You win a fee arbitration when you have a clean file which clearly shows the necessity of the work you did, the reasonableness of the time you allocated to doing it, and the fact that you advised the client in writing if you felt

---

25 Remember, as a young associate in a traditional firm, I had a quota for billable hours.

the time a particular issue or task he was demanding was not an effective use of your time and of his litigation budget.

On the other hand, I once won a fee arbitration when my former client was represented by a lawyer (not a family lawyer) who challenged (among other things) my time entry for two hours writing a case plan at the commencement of a very complex case with an estate worth several million dollars. He demanded to know how I could in conscience bill for writing a plan for the case at a time when I hadn't yet received the response to my petition for dissolution. After pointing out that a family law response form contains virtually no useful information except the alleged date of separation, I told the arbitration panel that the beginning of the case is the only sensible time to do the plan. If I didn't have a road map of where I was going at the beginning, how would I be able to effectively develop the case? I told them that the fact that I did early case plans was one of the reasons I was so effective and had developed the reputation I had, and which presumably was one of the reasons my client had retained me in the first place. I made it clear to the arbitration panel (which included two non-lawyers) that I thought this particular task was an essential part of complex family law litigation and I wasn't going to change my practice for this or any other client. I was awarded every penny I had billed.

What if the person you work for only gives you lousy cases to work on?

It goes without saying that the lawyer who does this is a dreadful business person, who probably compounds it by setting a billable hour quota, then downgrading your annual performance evaluation because of your high accounts receivable. I can't say I have a magic answer. The best suggestion is to memo the boss about why you think the case is a bad/unprofitable one. Keep a copy of the memo for yourself in case it disappears, don't put the memo in the client file, and then make sure you do the best damn work you can while working on an exit strategy.

Twelve

What to do when you think you've screwed up

Y ou will. It isn't a question of "if" but of "when."

Don't turn the file into the green monster on the side of your desk. Deal with it immediately. After all, you'll be losing sleep over it anyway, so it might as well be for real things you might still be able to fix, rather than fear and speculation about all the things you *might* have done wrong and are afraid to acknowledge. Avoidance is a very primitive and usually ineffective coping mechanism.

Do the research immediately to determine whether you in fact blew it and what might be done to fix/mitigate it while there is still time.

If you're an employee, tell your boss, (after you've done the research on your own). She may have other suggestions about how to handle it. If you're on your own, this is the time to call a more experienced lawyer who might have other suggestions on what you might do to fix it.

If you can't fix it, fess up to your client. We're all human, and I don't think it pays to pretend that we're perfect. That is simply an invitation to the client to sue you to prove that you're not. If you blew it, like as not, he knows it.

He also knows you are new and presumably consciously made that bargain in exchange for a lower hourly rate. That's not an excuse for malpractice, but it's a reason not to pretend you know it all. You don't. In fact, you never will. You'll just know a lot more than you know now.

You will eat your fee for what you screwed up, and the time you spend fixing it. So be it. And surprisingly, sometimes all the client will want is an honest apology.

You haven't a clue how to do something you need to do

This will be happening a lot for a while. Don't fall into the trap that many new lawyers do of either putting it off or trying to wing it to prove how brilliant you are. I don't care if you were tops in your class. Most of what it takes to be a good lawyer is entirely new to you. If you don't know how to do it, do the research. That's what you were trained to do. If you still don't know, figure out who *does* know, ask them, and then do what they suggest. If necessary, do your own independent research to verify the advice they've given you, but do it.

What if you are really stuck and don't have an in-house mentor?

If you really need to consult on a case, find an experienced lawyer whose opinion you respect and pay her for a case consultation. If your client is willing to pay for a second opinion, great. If it's just because you are still learning, pay for it yourself. It's an educational expense. Many experienced lawyers are glad to occasionally be a sounding board for a promising new lawyer. However, if you pay him for his time, you're more likely to get a thoughtful, complete response than if your colleague is being asked to give freebie advice while he's rifling through the stack of phone calls he has to return as soon as he can get you off the phone.

A question is only stupid if you have to ask it more than once.

What if the person who is paying your bill isn't the client?

They will often want to call the shots. This happens when Daddy calls to make an appointment for his kid's divorce. He makes a point of telling you that the bills should be sent to him. He then shows up with his kid for the first appointment. That part is easy. If you let him participate in the interview your attorney/client privilege is probably waived, so you explain to him that he can't stay or you won't be able to protect the confidentiality of your communications with his kid from the opposing spouse. Make him wait outside.

It gets harder when Daddy wants to call the shots in the divorce, set the strategy, and second guess what you are doing. It is critical that you make it clear that the *kid* is your client, not Dad. What you may find out is that the kid's idea of how the case should go is different from Dad's, and this situation is fraught with potential conflict. Sometimes your client doesn't *want* to do what Daddy wants, but is afraid to tell him directly. That means that your client hides behind you and you may get a nasty call from Dad. All you can really do in that situation is remind Dad that kid is your client and you really can't discuss it with him.

I once had a client who was the daughter of a very prominent local litigation attorney. He called to interview me before the consultation. It was a very civil conversation. It was clear that the case was going to be extremely messy and he wanted to be sure his daughter was going to be well cared for. Any parent would want the same. I assured him that I understood. Although I was a partner in my firm by then, I was still pretty young, and no doubt looked like a baby to him. I also told him that if his daughter retained me, there was something he could do to make the experience better for her. He should remember to wear his father hat, and not his litigator hat, when she talked to him about the case. I pointed out to him that he couldn't be objective about his own daughter, especially when he felt she was getting emotionally beaten up by a crazy husband. The case went very well, and the lawyer called me after it was done, complimented me on the job I did, and reported to me that my advice to him had made it easier for him to remain a resource for his daughter.

What if your client wants you do to something you feel is inappropriate?

If it's downright unethical, I hope you know what to do with that. If it is just inappropriate, and you tell them so, they usually say something like, "I'm paying you so you have to do what I say." My response to that was always "No, I'm a professional, but not *that* kind of professional. You need to find yourself the other kind."[26]

What if your boss instructs you to do something you don't think is ethical?

Don't do it.

You're the one who will get in trouble with the State Bar, not your boss.

You're the one whose license may be placed at risk.

You're the one whose professional reputation will suffer.

And start looking around for another boss.

What if you're well into the case and realize that your client really is "the bad guy"?

If there are no kids, it's unpleasant, but not the end of the world. Paper your file impeccably, do the best job you can, and get out at the earliest time you can safely do so, recognizing that the earliest time might not be until the end of the case.

If there are kids, it's tougher. Sometimes you fear that you will lose a meritorious custody case because you don't have much experience. That's bad. As you hone your skills, it may become fear that you read your client wrong, and because you're so very good at what you do, you win for the bad guy and some

---

26 The kind term is "hired gun;" the not so kind one is "whore." No one will respect you if you are either.

kid is scarred for life. Either will have you pacing the floor in the wee hours. I don't have an easy answer for this one. What I learned to do is use a different and much higher standard in screening clients for custody issues, just because I felt I had a higher duty to kids.

This may be one of the times when, after the case is over, you talk to the judge. When I was a young lawyer, I once had a client who presented very well and was quite credible. Dad accused her of alienating the kids, but I didn't see the signals and didn't believe him. She ended up skipping the country with the kids. I was devastated about the role which I had unwittingly played. A few weeks later I ran into the judge in the hallway and told him how terrible I felt. He was a kind and experienced judge who assured me that I had done my job professionally and that I wasn't responsible for not having predicted that my client would violate court orders and kidnap the kids.

The reality is that you will be representing some bad guys. You are an advocate and are not relieved of your professional responsibilities to your client because you find out he is a reprehensible human being. Take a page out of criminal defense lawyers' book, and remind yourself that you are doing it to preserve the integrity of the legal system and to ensure that everyone's rights are protected, and not for an individual client. You are still an officer of the court with a professional duty to your client.

The family you can't fix

We all want to help people or we wouldn't have chosen this field of law. Sometimes we'll be drawn to help someone out of a truly toxic situation. Sometimes your client's or the children's safety is at risk. It happens. It is a fact of life. It's just that in our line of work, we are more likely to be brought face to face with it. We'll try our damndest to help, but we don't always succeed.

What I'm going to tell you is hard to accept, but it must be said. Sometimes, no matter what you do and how competently you do it, someone is going to get hurt. Sometimes they may even get killed. Just because you got that restraining order doesn't mean that a true lunatic isn't going to violate it. I know a lawyer who tried to get a restraining order keeping a father away from his wife and kids. She filed for an *ex parte* restraining order without a hearing. The judge denied the order *ex parte* and set it for hearing in a week. Before the hearing date rolled around, that father not only killed his wife, but kidnapped the children, ultimately killing them and himself after a police standoff that lasted hours, ensuring that the final hours of those children's lives were filled with unspeakable horror. Both the judge who denied the order *ex parte* and the lawyer who asked for it will take those memories to their graves. Every family law judge I know has a similar story or knows someone who does. They agonize over how to tell the true crazy from the garden variety restraining order, based solely on the story they are told, and they don't have a crystal ball.

Just as I will take to my own grave the glow of the handful of cases where I know that I made a difference in a child's life, and that, because of my being there and doing the right thing at the right time, some kid was saved from a malignant parent, we also take the others with us. That goes with the territory. We're not going to win every battle that we should, and people are going to get hurt. That's why we always try to do the best job we can. We never know in advance which one it is going to be.

The truth is that there are truly crazy people out there, cruel parents, bitter, vengeful and dangerous losers. There are kids and clients who can't be saved. If you're not willing to take the risk that one of them might cross your path someday, you don't belong in family law. Go write real estate contracts, or litigate construction defects instead.

Protecting yourself

Sometimes the target of the crazy person will be *you*. After all, everything was just fine until their spouse came to you, and you got the restraining order which prevented them from conducting business as usual by tormenting her. It is almost universal that an abuser whose mate finally starts asserting legal rights will blame the lawyer who is protecting her. They will demonize you, because you are standing between them and their target. Some of these people are very, very crazy.

I've talked before about setting boundaries with clients. This is another reason to preserve some privacy and anonymity. Most of the time they just threaten, but you don't want this case to be the exception. I think it is just good business to keep your home phone unlisted[27] and maintain the privacy of your personal life. Of course, anyone who really wants to find you needs go no farther than Google, but you don't need to make it easy.

Although the person who stalked me was my own crazy ex-client, it could as well have been any one of a dozen angry opposing parties who blamed me for separating him from the target of his abuse. I've had my share of threats, and someone I helped put into San Quentin for three years for spousal battery told me I'd be the first person he looked for when he got out. Imagine my feelings when I moved into a gated community for the express purpose of obtaining some insulation from my stalker, only to find that my ex-client, the spouse of Mr. San Quentin had bought the house next door, and he would be coming to my street to pick up the kid for visitation? Fortunately, by that time, enough years had passed that he didn't recognize me when he pulled up in front of my house.

Our training and instincts are to protect our clients. That being said, there are limits. When I was a young lawyer, there was a very disturbing court incident. This was long before perimeter screening and security in court buildings. They were open to anyone, and anyone could bring a gun into court. A young family lawyer was representing her client when the opposing party, who had just lost, pulled out a gun and aimed it at his wife. I'm sure she was acting on instinct and didn't really think about it, but the lawyer stepped in front of her client, shielding her. The lawyer got shot.

The point is that our job is to do our legal best for our clients, not to take a bullet for them. I know lawyers who have had their cars run off the road,

---

27 One security expert I know lists his phone under the name of his pet, and recommends everyone have phone numbers listed under an alias.

who have had their homes vandalized, and or otherwise been threatened or physically accosted by their client's spouse. Be careful. It is only common sense to take threats seriously. Alert the bailiff if you suspect a security issue. There's no shame in asking the bailiff to walk you or your client to your car after court if you suspect the other party is dangerous and might confront you. And if I believed that the opponent was truly a threat to myself or my family, I'd report the problem to the police and get out of the case. I don't know a better reason to file a motion to withdraw, and can't imagine that any judge I know would deny it.

Thirteen

Your Legacy

So, let's come back to the question I asked at the beginning: What kind of family lawyer do you want to be?

Lawyers can be a pretty arrogant breed. Try to aim for humor and self confidence instead.

Ask yourself who you want to see in the mirror 25 years from now. That will help keep you focused on the practices and conduct most likely to produce the result you want.

What is your legacy? Are you going to leave the practice better than you found it? How?

Lawyers are often cynical. Some of this goes with the territory. You'll be seeing some really bad people doing really, really bad things. You will be seeing good people at their worst, in emotional crisis. These things can be painful to watch. Some lawyers choose to protect themselves by becoming cynical. If you want to be at the top of your profession, and have any quality of life, resist the temptation. Yes, there will be some painful experiences. However, there is nothing to equal the rush you will get from knowing you did a stellar job for someone who really needed you, and whose life (or whose children's lives) were permanently and positively impacted by you. Every case won't feel this way, but if you do it right and retain your ability to remember why you chose this work in the first place, you will not let the bad guys trick you into believing that there aren't any good guys.

Set your boundaries, don't take it home, and make sure that there is room in your life for the activities, causes, and hobbies that give it meaning. That will keep you in touch with your essential humanity, even in the face of people who sometimes do inhumane things, and will make it more likely that you really will change peoples' lives for the better. What more can we ask of our work?

What will you teach new lawyers when it is your turn? Think about it as you are learning yourself. With luck, you'll have lots of opportunities to pass on the wisdom you've learned to someone coming up behind you. It doesn't take much time to have a major impact on a new lawyer's professional career. I dedicated this book to two older lawyers who each took me aside at the courthouse to talk to me about professional courtesies, courtroom tactics, and building a professional reputation. Both were people I had opposed in court the day they took me aside. Neither spent more than forty-five minutes with me, but the insights they shared changed the trajectory of my legal career.

When your boss, opposing counsel or the judge abuses you, stop grinding your teeth long enough to promise yourself that when you are in her position, you'll do it differently. Remember how it felt to be on the receiving end and vow to do better when your time comes. Even better, develop some strategies now, while it is still fresh, so you know exactly *how* you could do it differently.

How will you leave the system better than you found it? Legal institutions are always evolving. The legal culture I cut my teeth in is entirely different from the legal culture I was trying cases in ten years later, different still from two years ago, or the cases I'm judging now. It will be evolving long after you retire.

When you have an opportunity to leave the law a little better than you found it, take advantage of it. It may not come again.

And whether you are at the top of the professional game, or on your way up, take a moment to look back down the path and offer assistance and encouragement to someone following behind. It only takes once to make a profound difference in someone's professional development. Never underestimate the importance of a kind word and gentle encouragement to a new lawyer. Pass on the gift.

About the Author

M Sue Talia started out in Danville, California, as a law clerk, then associate, then partner in a large general service law firm. After a number of years as a partner, she determined that the family law practice was an uncomfortable fit with the administrative needs of other areas of practice, and left to form her own firm, devoted exclusively to family law. She had a high end practice specializing in complex family law litigation.

Some years thereafter, she decided that she wanted to practice part time. Colleagues told her that a part time practice was incompatible with the high profile cases she handled. Her response was "watch me." Then over a period of two years, and through a process of trial and error, she developed and implemented a system for conducting a very profitable part time family law practice. The methodology she developed became the basis for her popular workshop "How to Have a Law Practice *AND* a Life."

With the time freed from the practice of law, she began writing and publishing books.[28] That led naturally to an involvement in legal reform activities which she continues to pursue.

---

28 *How to Avoid the Divorce from Hell (and dance together at your daughter's wedding)* (Third edition 2016), *A Client's Guide to Limited Legal Services* (1997), *Unbundling Your Divorce: How to Find a Lawyer to Help You Help Yourself* (2006) *Uncoupling in Three-Quarter Time: Life Affirming Divorce Poetry* (originally published in 2007 as *Divorce Chronicles*), as well as numerous articles.

Since 1997, she has limited her practice to private judging in complex family law matters. She continues to travel and write extensively, and is a national leader in the field of limited scope representation (sometimes called "unbundling").

Along the way, she has mentored numerous young family lawyers.

She lives in Danville, California, with her partner, Lee, and Rusty, their rescue Cairn terrier.

www.ingramcontent.com/pod-product-compliance
Lightning Source LLC
Chambersburg PA
CBHW032001190326
41520CB00007B/314